HOW TO HIDE
ANYTHING

HOW TO HIDE ANYTHING

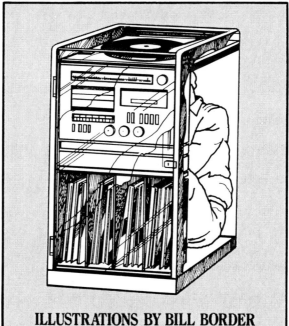

ILLUSTRATIONS BY BILL BORDER

MICHAEL CONNOR

PALADIN PRESS
BOULDER, COLORADO

How to Hide Anything
by Michael Connor

Copyright © 1984 by Michael Connor

ISBN 10: 0-87364-289-9
ISBN 13: 978-0-87364-289-7
Printed in the United States of America

Published by Paladin Press, a division of
Paladin Enterprises, Inc.
Gunbarrel Tech Center
7077 Winchester Circle
Boulder, Colorado 80301 USA
+1.303.443.7250

Direct inquiries and/or orders to the above address.

Illustrations by Bill Border

Visit our Web site at www.paladin-press.com

CONTENTS

INTRODUCTION

As GOVERNMENT IMPOSES MORE AND MORE RE-
strictions on what we can—or, more importantly, cannot—own; as the number of burglaries soar; as terrorism
by aberration or by design escalates; and as the possibility
of anarchy seems closer to home than ever, the need for
having a safe space for goods and persons becomes
pressing. Here are the guidelines to the design, selection,
and construction of hidden storage areas small enough
to hide cash and jewelry and large enough to conceal
armaments and ammunitions or, in the extreme, a family.

Before you begin lifting floorboards and hollowing walls,
you must first define what types of goods you will be
concealing from whom. How much forewarning will you
require to utilize the space—a knock at the door or a news
bulletin that the country has gone to war? Do you expect
to be searched by authorities possessing the latest in
detection training and devices, by roving renegades, or
by a team of professional burglars? And how much time
and money do you want to spend preparing your safe
spaces? All these questions must be considered first. Then
you will able to adapt the designs in this book for almost
any budget, structure, and need.

A good friend of mine sums it all up when he says, "If it's not nailed down, it's mine. And if I can pry it loose, it's not nailed down!" To get in the right frame of mind when you're surveying your place for possible stash areas, consider, if you will, where does a burglar first look for valuables? Probably in the safe, which kind of defeats its purpose, doesn't it? Sometimes the most obvious is also the least obvious. Just keep in mind that old adage about not being able to find something "right under your nose."

1. HOME-BASE HIDES

IT'S LATE AT NIGHT AND YOU AND THE WIFE ARE watching the evening news when you hear footsteps on the back porch. You're not expecting anyone at that hour and your heart pounds with dread. You've already stashed your really important papers and cash in a place you're certain no one will ever look, but your wallet is stuffed with the proceeds from your just-cashed paycheck, your wife's rings are worth over a thousand dollars (not to mention the sentimental value), and your watch is a keepsake from your dead father. How can you protect them in a hurry from burglars?

The easiest way to find the best locations for quick hiding places for small items such as cash, watches, and jewelry is to sit yourself down in your home, retreat, or office and have a good look around. Unless you are a caveman, chances are there will be dozens of usable areas. Let's start with the most obvious.

Modern, mass-produced covered chairs, sofas, and ottomans disassemble easily and reassemble quickly without showing signs of tampering and can be fitted with easily accessible hidden pockets. The staples, screws, or pins used to secure the upholstery to the underside of the unit's frame can be removed or loosened, depending

1

If the hide is to be used regularly, press-stud fastenings can be substituted for some of the staples.

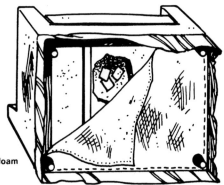

Underside of chair showing material pulled back to reveal stash hidden in foam

on what you want to hide. Most such furniture contains vast amounts of foam rubber, padding, and stuffing. It is a simple matter to cut out cavities, secure with double-sided tape or adhesive, and refit. A cheap staple gun, obtainable from the hardware store, will make your job look professional. Always make sure that enough foam or padding is replaced over the goods to give the correct feel to the chair in case it is poked and prodded during a search.

The design of some such furniture enables objects to be simply pushed down between the framework and the covering. If you have had loose change drop from a pocket into such a chair, you will know the hassle in trying to retrieve it without disassembling the unit. Thieves may slash the furniture, but it is unlikely that they will thoroughly examine the insides.

The "antiquey" wooden furniture popular today is also very useful for hide construction. The kind of chair shown below is easily taken down to its component form, and

Leg drilled out to reveal cavity

A rubber hammer used for panel beating is handy.

the separate pieces can then be drilled to take goods. Unless the chair or table is of very substantial manufacture, its various parts will probably be held together with powerful glue. If trouble is encountered in removing the legs, uprights, and so on, apply quantities of hot water or, if available, wood glue softener. A combination of the two will do the trick. Bore out adequate space for your items, but do not weaken any pieces that will have to carry considerable weight. Ladderback chairs and gateleg tables are obviously the first choice for such alteration. Using a household drill and bit, the job only takes a few minutes. For long-term concealment, add plenty of adhesive when reassembling. The hide will stand up to all normal checks with ease.

Hi-fi speakers, which come in a number of useful shapes and sizes, are easily opened and stashed with goods in a matter of minutes. Rather than give a list of similar hides, it is sufficient to say that any piece of furniture or home equipment that can be opened can also be used to conceal goods. Remember, however, that if a criminal search takes place, there is a chance that the very articles containing goods will be stolen. A nice surprise for the thief should he decide to open them up!

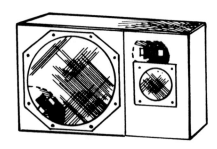

The electric light switch on the wall is easily removed simply by undoing a couple of screws. Always turn the main power off first, of course. The available space at the back of the switch plate will vary from place to place, but you will generally be able to conceal at least a few items. If you are hiding metal objects make sure they are well insulated to avoid the possibility of a short circuit.

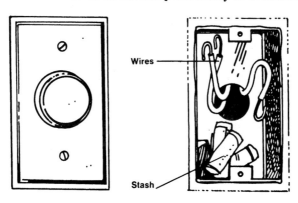

The electric outlet, or wall plug, is removed just as simply, and will reveal a surprising amount of space. Apply the same precautions as for the switch. In a lot of instances, it will be found that the socket housing is

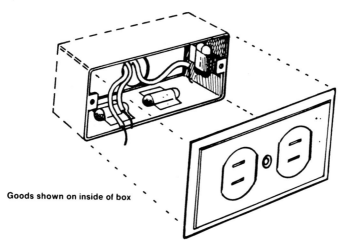

Goods shown on inside of box

readily removed from the wall, and you then have access to the space between the plaster and the brickwork.

When reassembling, do a tidy job making sure that no traces of brick dust are left in the area. As an extra measure, add a coat of paint to the unit, making sure that it covers the screw heads. (Most poor decorators do this anyway, and it causes problems when the need to remove the socket cover arises). The plastic type of covers fade after a time, and painting them is not uncommon. A more elaborate method of using the wall socket is given in chapter two.

For small items an electric plug itself can be quickly adapted. Simply open the plug up, and remove the fuse and wire connectors. The internal moldings can be filed down or burnt away with a hot knife.

If more room is required, take the following steps. Remove the legs of the plug—these simply pull out—and, using a hacksaw, cut three parts of their length off, as shown. Replace the legs and secure using a strong ad-hesive. The plug can be reassembled with the goods inside and plugged into the wall socket as usual. As a safety precaution, it may be better to remove the main fuse that links the power to that particular plug, although if the stash is well insulated with plastic tape there should be no problem.

The false-bottom drawer or cupboard is still a useful way of quickly stashing some items. Don't be greedy and try to block off 90 percent of the drawer's total area; err on the side of caution. Use several narrow hides rather than one large, obviously altered one. Drawers and cup-boards so converted should contain plenty of junk.

Drawers are likely to be pulled out and tipped up during a search, whether by crooks or the authorities, and a loosely fitted false bottom will just drop out. To fasten the false bottom securely, use velcro strips or magnets. (You can get really useful strip magnets from the plastic

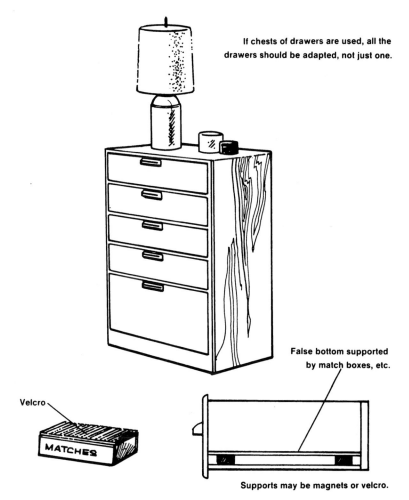

If chests of drawers are used, all the drawers should be adapted, not just one.

False bottom supported by match boxes, etc.

Velcro

MATCHES

Supports may be magnets or velcro.

door edges of the refrigerator.) Insert a metallic strip or plate somewhere beneath the base of the false boot so that you can lift out the unit. If you use magnets to retain the false base, make sure you can obtain a stronger magnet to lift the base out again. A magnet often sold as the Sea Search is very powerful and does a great job.

If you are converting a cupboard, you can get away with a less elaborate fixing system.

One of the first hiding places that springs to mind for concealing small objects around the house is the old hollow book. While the hollow book technique is useful for some applications (I would suggest its use in a library full of unconverted books of similar size and color), there are several ways to improve upon the basic idea.

Choose a good-sized book. Forget paperbacks and the like. Books with thin pages are to be favored, as such pages have a natural sticking tendency and add strength to the stash. Never start the hollow within the first few pages. Pick a point at least a third of the way into the book and make sure that the bottom of the hollow does not extend farther than a third of the way in from the end. That means effectively that the middle third of the book is used for the stash. The area of the hollow should

Only middle third used for stash

extend no farther than an inch and a half from the edge of the pages. This decreases the likelihood of the stash being found during a quick flip-through. The item itself should be securely fixed to the inside of the hollow, so that if the book is held upside down it will not drop out. The commonest form of book search (when several are to be examined) is to hold the book upside down and shake it.

Fancy curtain poles of the type shown below lend themselves readily to conversion. The metal pole will conceal more for a given length than the wooden one, and has the benefit of being already hollow. Items are just pushed or dropped into the pole, and the end piece is replaced. It is obvious, though, that the pole is hollow, and if a very tough search is anticipated, the wooden pole is a safer bet. Take care not to drill out too much of diameter of the pole; common sense will dictate when enough is enough. Always insert a plug of suitably colored material into the end of the pole before refixing the end piece. This plug, which conceals the cavity, can easily be made from plastic wood, or any similar substance. For added security, glue the end piece securely with adhesive. Use super glue and when the time comes to retrieve the items, apply the appropriate solvent, which is available from the place where the glue was purchased.

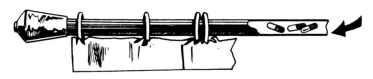

Inside of pole drilled out with large-diameter bit

If you plan to do some redecorating, the next technique is well worth thinking about. It requires the use of a router or other tool that will allow you to dig out a trench from the sheetrock plaster covering on your wall. Cut the trench to the desired depth and shape (backing brickwork can also be chipped away with a chisel), and attach a few clips or velcro pads to secure the goods in place. They will not be so large as to stand proud of the surrounding wall, and neither will the goods.

Once the stash is secured, affix a length of sheetrock, wallboard, or whatever you like. If the wall is of the old-fashioned plaster type, a thin skin of plaster to cover the hide is all that is needed, and probably all that the thickness of the surrounding plaster will allow. Repaper the wall or use veneer boards to complete the hide. If wallpaper is used, then on the section covering the hide apply spray-on artist's glue or rubber cement instead of paste. This will enable you to peel the paper away from

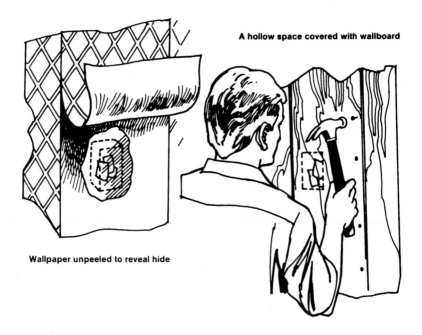

A hollow space covered with wallboard

Wallpaper unpeeled to reveal hide

the hide and then stick it down again. If wallboards (veneer boards) are used, then the screw fastenings (to batons on the wall) appear normal, yet allow for rapid access to the hide.

The fridge is very useful for concealing goods. The old favorite hiding place is in the freezer compartment inside a chicken or a pie or whatever. The whole lot freezes, and only a very determined search (or a chicken and pie thief) will uncover the stash.

Goods can be stashed in the freezer.

Also in the kitchen, the kickboard hide is worth a mention. These kickboards are the pieces of finishing wood or molding at the base of kitchen units, cabinets, and so on. The kickboard is easily removed for access to considerable space. The board can simply be nailed back into place and levered off when required. After a few times, the wood around the nails becomes worn enough to facilitate "on-offing" of the panel without it becoming noticeably loose. Magnets, velcro, sticky pads, and so on can also be used to secure the panel.

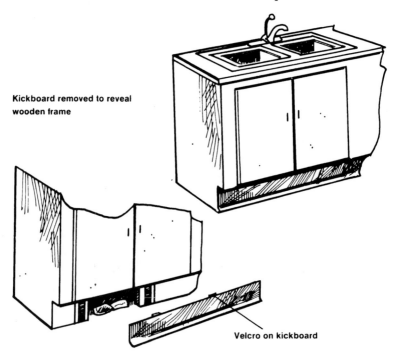

Kickboard removed to reveal
wooden frame

Velcro on kickboard

A pan of fat or a half-filled deep-fat fryer is innocent-looking enough, but can conceal a fair amount of jewelry. Simply heat some fat or solid vegetable shortening and, while it is still liquid but not too hot, insert the well-sealed goodies. The surface of the fat will settle into a smooth flat area when cooled and hardened, and the chances of your stash being suspected are remote.

Cutaway of pan showing items hidden in fat

A pot of food cooking on the stove is always a handy thing if you are expecting unwelcome visitors. Anything from an auto pistol to a pouch of uncut diamonds can be dropped in and left until the visit is over.

Other kitchen possibilities are bottles of frozen drink or milk. Place the item in the container, making sure it is well sealed, and simply pop into the fridge. Solid vegetable shortening, butter, or a hundred other foodstuffs will give the required amount of security. When selecting such hides, try to pick foods that are messy, impossible to examine without destroying, or very smelly (garlic

Always wrap or rewrap foodstuffs to add to the effect.

sausage or stilton cheese). Let us say these are just the tip of the iceberg—but they should give you food for thought!

An internal door is usually hollow—a sandwich of hardboard or ply with no filling. Using only the simplest tools, a cavity can be cut into the top, side, or bottom of the door as shown. Some doors may contain a fire retardant material or a woodchip substance. Either way it can still be easily cut out to create useful space. A lid can be made from a slice of wood fixed in place with pins or small magnets. In some cases, removing the lock mechanism will allow access to the inside of the door.

The door frame itself, depending on construction, can be partially removed and the brickwork behind it altered to take a stash. You could chip out part of a brick or chisel away a whole one. In older houses, the securing door nails are easily pried out and then simply pushed

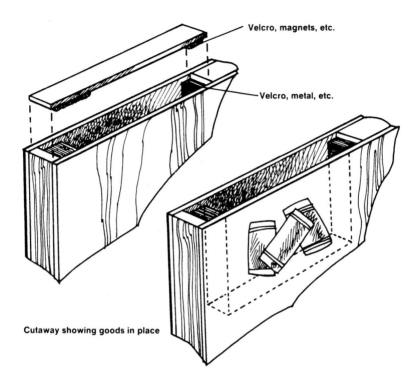

Velcro, magnets, etc.

Velcro, metal, etc.

Cutaway showing goods in place

back into place with little or no loss of strength. A complete false frame can be made and secured with any fastening that permits easy access to the hide.

Most staircases can be quite easily adapted to provide room for and ready access to a good-sized hide. Usually the hardest work involved here is removing part of the plasterboard backing that is often affixed to the underside of the staircase. Your selected vertical length is removed, either by cutting or loosening, depending on the design of the staircase, and a hinge assembly attached as shown. Some form of securing system is affixed to the bottom of the vertical length and its corresponding position on the adjoining horizontal length. If it is necessary to cut through the vertical length, the drilling of a row of holes

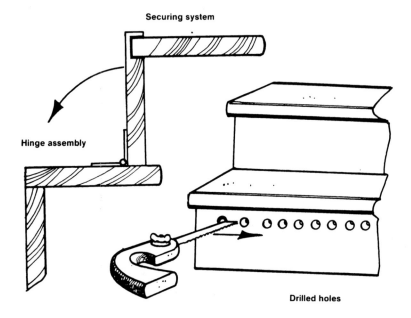

first, as shown, saves a lot of time and trouble. Watch the weight of your cache if the staircase backing is plasterboard, and use stair carpet or whatever to add that extra touch of camouflage.

The undersides of staircases in most buildings are used as storage space. These are obviously one of the first places that any experienced person conducting a search would look, so, if you do construct a hidden area in such a location, pay great attention to detail. The quickest method of "losing" part of the understair cupboard area is to construct a simple frame affair as shown, around the edge of which are hammered in a quantity of broad-headed nails.

Next, measure up a piece of suitably colored plaster-board or whatever, and affix several small magnets to its outer edge. A coat rack or any similar assembly is fixed to the makeshift wall for a handle to lift the wall into position. Use long screws to hold the coat rack in place. If the wall has to be secured from the inside, a backing block of the type illustrated can be employed. The long timber overlaps the frame edge by a few inches, and the holes drilled in it allow the coat rack screws to penetrate it. A smaller lock block is then screwed home over the protruding screws as shown, securing the 'wall' etc. rigidly. If longer than required screws are used, and instructions for the "backing block" technique shown in the hidden room section followed, the understair cupboard can also be used for hiding personnel. In this case, make sure it can be locked from the inside.

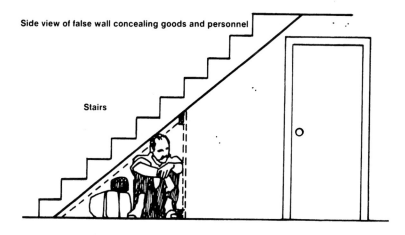

Side view of false wall concealing goods and personnel

Stairs

If you have a garden, the next hide is really great, and if you happen to be a fisherman as well, perfect! All you do is seal the goodies well in water- and rotproof material, a plastic container for example, and place it at the bottom of the garden. Next cover it with rotten vegetables, leaves and so on. A plastic compost bin can be purchased to keep things under control. In next to no time you will have the most valuable compost heap in the city! Few people will willingly poke around in such muck, and retrieval is accomplished simply by raking and tending

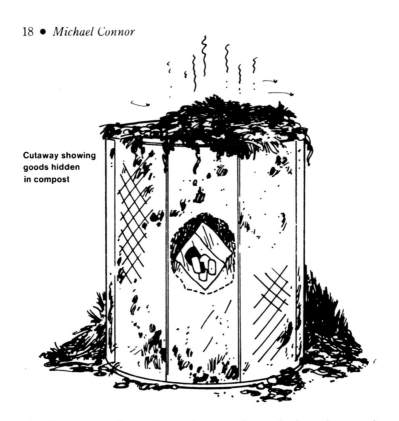

Cutaway showing goods hidden in compost

the heap as all good gardeners do and then barrowing away the cache under a spadeful of compost. Anyone watching you will not become as suspicious as if you were simply to bury and dig up items every few days.

Buy two compost bins while you're at it, and put one at the other end of the garden. Into this beauty sling a couple of pounds of rotting meat. Your well-wrapped valuables are placed in the bin as well. Leave the lid off for a few days so that the sun and the flies can do their stuff. In a short time the bin will be crawling with filthy, disgusting maggots (for your fishing of course!). Anyone who is prepared to grovel around up to his elbows in maggots deserves your stash, so hand it over with a smile. Once you have a useful amount of maggots, put a lid on the bin to keep the number of plague deaths in the neighborhood to a minimum.

A variation is to start an insect farm, take up snake collecting, or purchase a tank of pirhana fish! I know a guy who has a pet Portuguese man-of-war, an evil looking jellyfish. He keeps his month's supply of coke (not cola) in the bottom of the tank in a little plastic box covered by colored gravel. He knows where the stash is and can fish it out easily, but who in his right mind would want to tangle with a jellyfish? One day the jellyfish will find the coke, and that really will be something to see! Anyway, I'm sure you get the idea: Unpleasant usually equals unsearched.

The room may contain any one of a variety of air vents, air conditioning units, or heating outlets, and items simply placed inside such openings will usually pass unnoticed. Most of the covers or grilles for these vents are removed easily with a screwdriver. Secure the item with tape or adhesive.

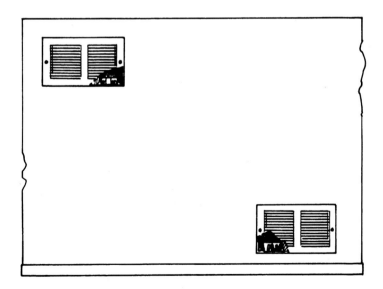

Affix to inside of vent with adhesive, magnet, etc.

A nice variation on this is to affix a hinge to the grille, as shown, and then, in turn, to the wall. The grille can then be opened door-fashion whenever it is needed. Always replace the screws, which can be shortened by cutting if necessary, to give the impression of a tightly fastened cover.

A simple under-floor hide is often used, and while such hiding places are convenient and effective, it is worth paying attention to the following points.

When using such a hide, choose a position that is not at, or close to, the edge of the floor area. Although it is tempting to just roll back the carpet a foot or so before prying up a floor board, anyone searching thoroughly will do the same. It is unlikely, however, that the center of the floor will be examined. It takes a little longer to effect this hiding place, but it is worth it.

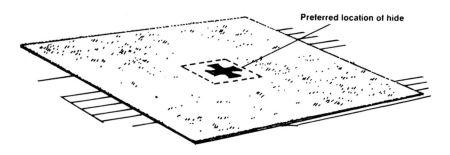

Preferred location of hide

Edge of carpet will probably be lifted during a search.

Always have plenty of furniture in the room, and, if possible, over the spot covering the hide. If, however, the furniture looks odd or out of place, leave the area bare.

Remember not to overdo the weight of items hidden in this manner if the floor is a ceiling as well—especially if it is someone else's ceiling! As a security measure, affix the goods to the side of a floor beam rather than simply placing them between beams. On the ground floor of most buildings there is usually a surprising amount of space between the floor and the footings. Replace boards carefully and avoid breaking them at all costs, as the resulting fresh wood is a dead giveaway in the event of the carpet being lifted and the floor examined.

Many thick, heavy-pile carpets have a backing that can be readily loosened or split to give a glove effect. Items are simply pushed inside and the opening sewn or glued back together. The stash is suitable for papers, cash, or powders. I have seen a carpet, doctored in the way shown, thrown to one side during a search with no thought for its content. Providing the goods hidden are of a sensible shape and size, I recommend this method.

Most UHF/VHF antennas are of a tubular aluminum construction and have end pieces capped with small plastic plugs. These plugs are easily pried out with a knife or screwdriver, and items can then be inserted. When the antenna is mounted in a loft or on the roof, the mast can also be utilized with great effect. If mounting outside, ensure that adequate weatherproofing precautions are taken; plastic bags do nicely.

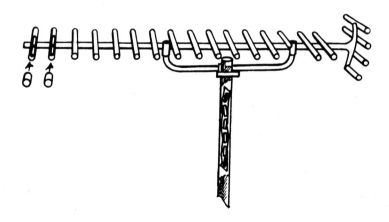

When you're in the loft, have a look at the insulation. Thick fiberglass insulation is easily pulled apart and goods can be concealed. In some of the thicker insulation, armaments can be secured providing, of course, that no one lifts up the fiberglas mat. This technique is more effective than just putting the goods under the insulation, but always wear gloves, as the material causes itching and skin irritation among many people. This factor, combined with dust and poor light, effectively deters all but the most determined of examiners from looking for too long or too closely in such an area.

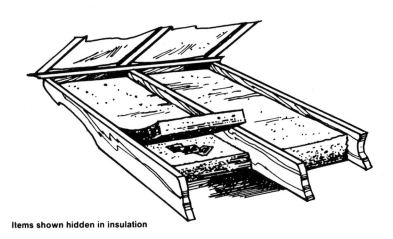

Items shown hidden in insulation

2. ELABORATE HIDING PLACES

Hiding larger items such as handguns, shotguns or ammo takes more thought and more elaborate arrangements. Not only do you have to anticipate concealing the length, you must also take into consideration the weight. One of the easiest types of larger stashes is dummy pipework added to existing pipes or ductwork. The fake pipe, while appearing genuine even under close inspection, actually contains secreted goods. Bathrooms, toilets, and anywhere else that contains quantities of pipes or ductwork are the first choice.

Plastic tubing, available from any hardware store in a variety of lengths and shapes, and with a whole range of end caps and the like, can be utilized with great effect in these areas. At the simple end of the scale, merely add a length of tube, suitably painted to match the rest of the pipework, in any desired location. The diagram following shows a length of dummy pipe in place. It is secured simply by cutting out a hole of the correct diameter at each end of the selected location. The pipe just rests in place and can be removed quickly.

Many of the partition walls in modern buildings are sheetrock, not heavy brickwork. In fact, none but the main walls will be made from substantial brick. Even the

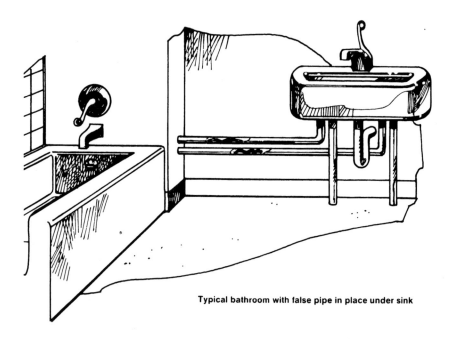

Typical bathroom with false pipe in place under sink

lightweight blocks used in modern buildings can be cut with a simple handsaw or cut or scraped with a knife. A chisel, small hammer, or any other similar tool will speed up conversion jobs no end.

Shown below is the typical construction method employed by builders of modern, low level dwellings. Obviously, designs vary considerably, but the point of the diagram is to show that, generally speaking, a building has a substantial outer frame, and a considerably less solid internal structure that forms the inner walls. When this method is employed, there is always a gap between the inner and outer walls as shown. Access to this gap can be obtained in various ways depending on the type of building in question. Have a look around the inside and outside of a given wall to see if this technique has been used in the building's construction. In fact, if you can obtain an architect's plan of the property, the gaps between the inner and outer walls will be clearly marked.

You can then construct a suitable door into this gap using techniques in this book.

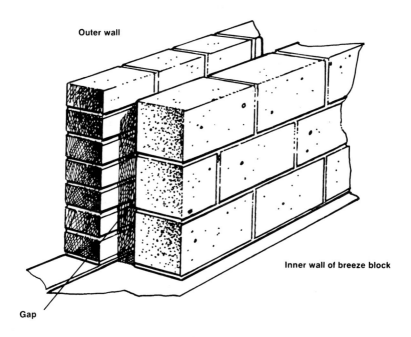

The tool shed or garage, if well equipped with tools, is probably the best place to start having a go at some basic conversion techniques. Spades, forks, rakes, and the like can all be turned into safe spaces by simply boring a channel inside of wooden handles. Metal-handled tools will probably be hollow anyway, saving any effort at all. The garden wheelbarrow, if of a tubular construction, can have items pushed inside with little difficulty, especially into the handle lengths. The tire can also be removed, items taped to the inside of the wheel, and the tire replaced. Always leave the tools in normal locations, and if unused equipment is doctored, make sure to roughen the appearance of the tool to give the impression of use.

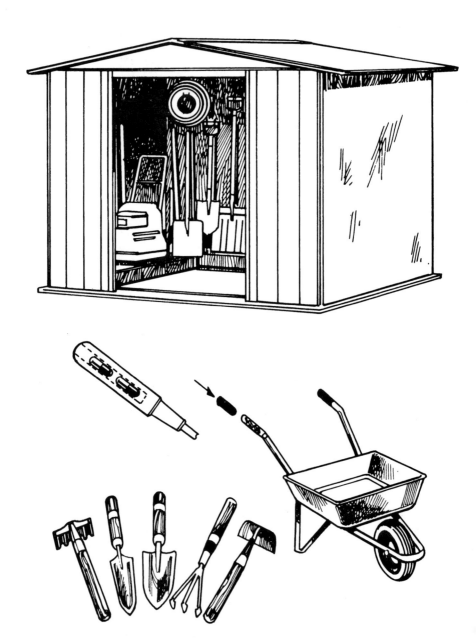

Various tools with handles drilled out

The elements of space heaters, whether ceramic or wire wound, will hold enough illegal substance to make the effort involved in adapting them well worthwhile. Simply remove the end cap connectors from the element, and plug one end with putty or the like. Insert the stuff to be hidden, refit both of the end caps and replace in the heater. As a safety precaution, remove the fuse that links the fire to the mains. Spare elements could be adapted

Hollow element

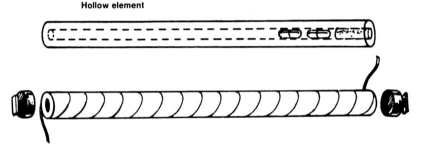

End connector

in this way and stored around the home without attracting suspicion. The hot water tank or water heater in most buildings takes the form of a large copper cylinder, in which is a heating element. With the aid of a small blowlamp and a heavy hand, it is possible to desolder the joint around the tank. Designs vary; some tanks may be two-piece, in which case the above method can be used to separate the two. In other cases it may be possible to remove the tank thermostat, the heater element connector unit, or some other part of the assembly that will give you access to the inside of the tank. In still water systems the water that fills the tank will not be in the loft but will sit atop the heater itself. This will have a removable lid allowing items, suitably wrapped, to be hung or dropped inside. There is usually enough play in the various joints of the connecting pipes to allow partial

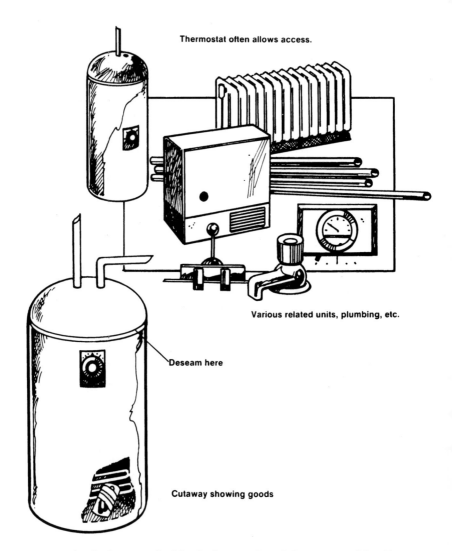

Thermostat often allows access.

Various related units, plumbing, etc.

Deseam here

Cutaway showing goods

removal of the top half of the tank with no trouble. It may, however, be necessary to take off any tightly fitted or restricting pipework connections.

It is likely that there will be a way to gain access to the inside of the tank, but the size of the opening will vary from model to model.

For a more professional hiding place, use an opening method that involves relatively simple procedures such as unscrewing the thermostat housing. The hide can then be opened and closed quickly with little fuss. As a safety precaution, remove the main power fuse linking the heater or take off a connection at the heater itself.

Remove any traces of tampering during refitting. Where desoldering is used to separate two halves of the tank, refit the pieces loosely enough to give ready access, but firmly enough to pass casual examination. Your chosen method will, of course, depend upon the purpose of the hide.

Plastic pipe can be obtained in large enough diameters to conceal quite sizable goods. Apart from disguising these as part of existing plumbing work, their use in the following manner is very effective. The method shown presumes the availability of an earthen floor, but with a little ingenuity you will be able to adapt the technique for specific requirements (as with all good ideas!).

Remove any carpet, tiling, or floor covering from the chosen area, once again selecting a place not within easy reach of the floor perimeter, just in case. Dig out enough of the earth to enable the container to be sunk level with the top of the hole, then give it a press with your foot so that it is an inch at most below the surface. Cover the container with soil, replace any covering, floorboards, or whatever, and tidy up. Make a note of the location of the hide, or hides, using a simple "five paces in, three to the right" system. All sorts of goodies can be stashed in plastic pipe with no damage from humidity or damp if tight-fitting screw-on end caps are used.

It is worth mentioning here that several publications detail ways of hiding metallic items so that a metal detector search comes up negative. They include such things as *chaff*—"foiling" the authorities by planting large quantities of aluminum wrap and the like to give the impression that a jumbo jet must be buried there. The operator, assuming a jumbo jet *couldn't* be buried there, supposedly gives up. Or, if using an area outside of the home to bury items, select a kennel yard, or arrange for animals to frequent the spot! The iron-rich urine has a blanketing effect on detection readings, and it is assumed the animals are solely responsible for the readings. Many other such tricks are cited. However, the operative word here is *metal* detector. The authorities in all but the most backward areas now have sophisticated "disturbance indication detectors" that will reveal irregularities in the ground where something is buried, whether or not it is metallic. These things are not foolproof, but it is worth remembering. Even less sophisticated devices, grouped wrongly under the label *metal detectors,* have extremely fine tuning facilities to enable the operator to tune out certain readings in an area and home in on one or two. Of course, this will only concern you if your intention is to defeat a police or other official search. The chances of rampaging thugs, rioters, and looters coming armed with such devices is, to say the least, remote.

An improvement on the simple electric socket stash shown in chapter 1 is obtained with a suitably sized cash box, strongbox, or whatever that has a frontal key locking system. Such boxes are available in a variety of sizes from many outlets. You should be able to get one that will fit into a hole slightly smaller than the cover plate of the electric sockets used in your home.

Quite simply, the front, or wall, plate of an electric socket unit is obtained and fitted to the front of the cash box, taking care that the box's lock is accessible via one of the plug-leg openings in the front plate. Minor alteration to the size of the plug-leg hole will probably be required, but this does not matter. Attach the plate using powerful epoxy adhesive.

The box is now fitted into the wall at a height and

in a location that matches the other electric sockets in the room. Secure the box well with cement. You now have a custom-built wall safe. As a finishing touch, attach a cut-down electric plug (shown in chapter 1) to the socket plate using sticky-back pads. The effort of removing and replacing these pads when using the safe is well worth the trouble.

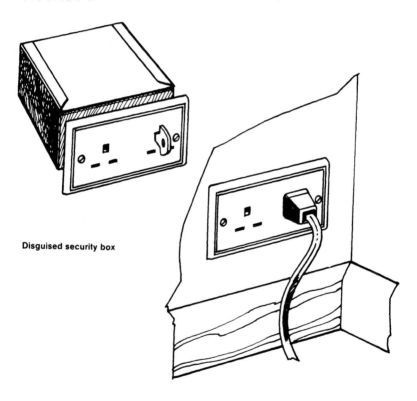

Disguised security box

If you find that one of the rooms you have access to has a long, vertical run of piping, such as a toilet down pipe, that can be disassembled at the top or at both top and bottom, then a quick way of concealing suitably sized items is as follows.

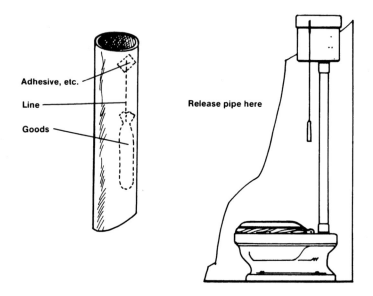

For convenience, remove the pipe at both ends. If this is not possible, simply removing the top connection will suffice. Wrap the goods in suitable material, and attach a length of fishing line, piece of wire, or whatever. The stash is then attached to the inside of the pipe as shown, using waterproof glue, and the pipe refitted. The water runs over the stash (assuming you have not overdone the diameter of the container) and the pipe appears perfectly normal, as indeed it is. Alternatively, the line or wire holding the stash can be wedged into the top connector during reassembly.

On a larger scale, the waste down pipe from the toilet can be disconnected and the same technique employed. Many toilet down pipes are what one might call *loose coupled,* and removing a few layers of tape bandage and a couple of screws gives ready access.

Outside drains, the covers of which are simply lifted out, will conceal a plastic pipe container which is secured to the drain cover in the same manner. Drain pipes (from

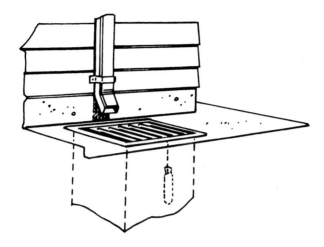

the roof guttering) which run down outside walls, hollow gateposts, and many similar structures can also be used with great effect.

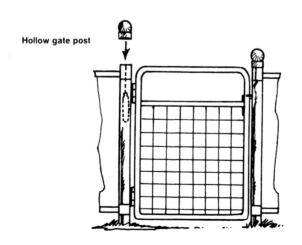

Hollow gate post

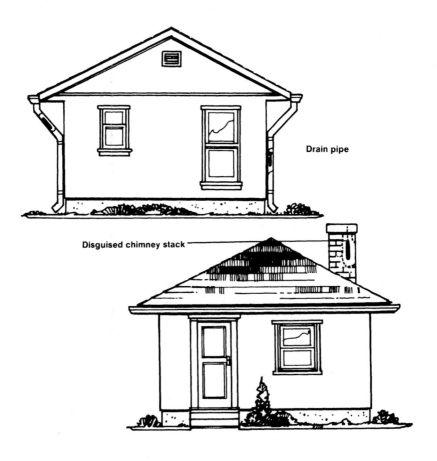

Drain pipe

Disguised chimney stack

The inside panel of fridges and freezers is usually of a plastic material and can be removed quite easily. Designs vary, but in most cases a few obviously placed screws are all that hold the plastic wall in place. Sometimes the screws are covered with a small, rounded "hat." These are easily pried off with a knife or screwdriver. The insulation material used in these units is even worse than the stuff used for loft insulation, and gloves should always be worn. The material is not harmful, but causes skin irritation.

Cutaway showing goods

Items can be packed in and around this insulation, and the plastic wall replaced. Sometimes there are no screws as such, but small plastic rivets instead. These are pried apart into a male and female pair. Removing the pieces of plastic wall that have trays and compartments molded into them will give considerable room for storage. There may also be available to you other similar domestic appliances that have removable or easily disassembled interior sections. Have a look around, but if you live with a person who is unaware of your activities, choose the location carefully!

Many rooms, hallways, and cupboards have some form of coat- or hat-hanging unit. The type shown below is very common, and if not already fitted, can be constructed

Wooden base (backboard)

in a matter of minutes. The chances are that this type of hanger or hook unit will be mounted to an internal wall that is constructed from plasterboard or the like. Behind it there will be only a number of supporting timbers and lots of safe space. The coathook backboard will probably be attached to a couple of the support timbers with nails or screws. Either way, it will be apparent during examination, and the backboard can be pried away from the timbers or unscrewed. Once this is done, an opening is cut in the wall, as shown.

Support timber into which the backboard is screwed

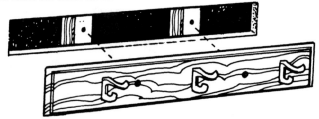

Hole cut out of plasterboard (sheetrock)

Items can be attached to the inside of the outside wall or the outside of the inside wall using tape, sticky pads, and so on. If regular use is to be made of the hide, a more elaborate system employing shelving, hooks, and so on could be installed.

To make access simple, neat, and safe, affix a couple of spring clips to the support timbers as shown below.

Magnets and metal strips could also be used.

Spring clips or other suitable attachment

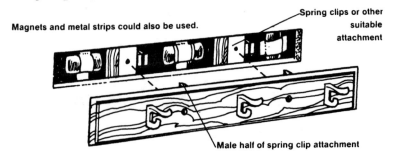

Male half of spring clip attachment

The entire assembly can be pushed home where it will stay, firmly held by the spring clips, and pulled away to reveal the hide when required. Any other form of fastening can be used, but consider the weight that the reassembled unit is going to have to take.

Many homes still have windows that operate on a sash principle. These are the kind of windows that stay open on their own when lifted into position. The weight of the window is counterbalanced by a weight that hangs, via a pully assembly, within the frame of the window itself.

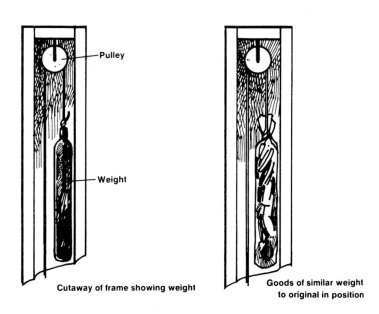

Cutaway of frame showing weight

Goods of similar weight to original in position

All you need to do to gain access to this space, which is quite substantial, is to carefully pry out the nails, screws, or whatever holds the frame cover in place. The weight will be clearly visible, and if a container is filled with goods of a similar total weight, the original can be removed and the container attached in its place.

Alternatively, simply secure items to the inside of the frame box, making sure that they do not interfere with operation of the window. There is one weight on either side of the window, and care should be taken when removing them to ensure that the window is shut. Unless, of course, you like very short, fat fingers!

The window ledge, or window sill, in many homes can be lifted away from its mounting with the help of a softheaded hammer. Depending on the construction of the building, it will be covering either a base of solid brickwork or (more likely) a space between two rows of brickwork. If the building is brick-built throughout, this will definitely be the case. Goods can be stashed in the opening, and the window ledge replaced. The original nails that secured the ledge should be discarded, and some other, less drastic, form of fixing employed to facilitate ease of removal in the future.

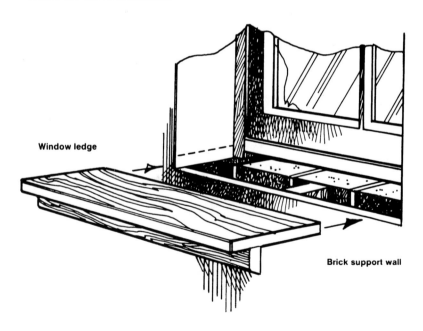

Window ledge

Brick support wall

Remember that house construction techniques differ so widely that this stash may not be practical for your needs. Some window sills are fixed to the innermost of two rows of brickwork, the window frame itself being atop the outermost. This is not always the case, however, so check it out before chopping it out. Have a wander around any nearby housing development and ask the workmen if they can tell you the basic design of the building in question. In my own home, which is actually a flat, the window ledge in the living room came away from the brick base with little difficulty. A sort of up-and-outward action was required to save the surrounding walls on either side from excessive damage, and the nails brought out a ton of brickdust. This was easily vacuumed away, and the evidence on the wall areas tidied up with plaster and cement. A good coat of paint covers any giveaway marks, and wallpaper to replace that damaged during sill removal is easy to obtain and hang!

Kitchen tabletops and counters can easily be turned into useful safe space. Most modern units will have a thin veneer covering on the edge which can be peeled off after being loosened with a knife. If difficulty is encountered, use the kettle to apply steam to the area to be loosened. The veneer strips are held only by adhesive,

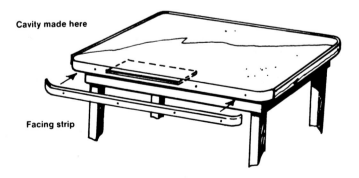

and the steam will soften it. (Occasionally a tack may have been inserted as well. Check first.)

Once the edge piece, or facing strip, is removed, a cavity can be cut or gouged out of the edge of the table- or countertop with a suitable tool. My favorite method for securing the facing piece back in position is to use spray-on rubber cement, or a couple of sticky-back pads that have been cut in half widthways to increase the chance of the facing piece making a flush contact to the edge. Magnets could also be used. A small pack of usefully sized magnets may be available from children's toy shops. They are very cheap, and come in a wide variety of shapes.

In many instances, the floor of the property you have access to will be concrete. At ground level or in the basement, this presents as much of a problem as you want it to. By that I mean should you consider that an under-, or rather, in-floor, hide is going to serve you best, then there are a few ways in which you can effect the conversion. The most apparent of these is the use of a router (easily rented for a few dollars if you don't own one) to cut out a trench from the concrete. The goods

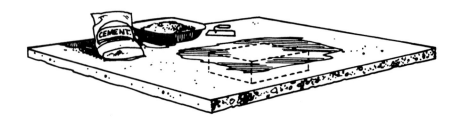

are well sealed, and a thin layer of concrete (or just cement) is skimmed over the hide as camouflage. Use dirt, dust and so on to finish the job and make sure that the newly worked area is not visible. Again, the easiest way is to have the goods in a solid-topped box which is buried so that its top is flush with the surrounding floor. The cement is then skimmed over it. Make a note of the hide's location; you will be surprised how easy it is to forget the exact point.

Alternatively, and recommended if the floor is above ground level, is the use of concentrated acid to eat a cavity out of the cement. In the tests I tried, concentrated nitric acid softened a foot square area of cement in a couple of hours. It was then possible to scrape out the debris. Always wear gloves, a face mask, and goggles or protective glasses. Apply the acid a few drops at a time, and scrape and poke at the area continually with a screwdriver or similar tool. A few problems can be encountered when trying to pull up floorboards unless you plan the job carefully before commencing.

A great many floorboards are fitted using what is called a tongue and groove method. This means that one board has a groove in it, and the next board in the row has a tongue, or protrusion, that fits into the groove. Many mistaken people dive straight in and try to lever up a centrally placed board, the result of which, if a tongue and groove technique has been used, is rapid destruction of the floorboard. *Always* start at an outer edge when lifting this type of board. I know it's a pain to have to lift thirty boards just to get at the one in the middle, but believe me, the finished job will be far superior and far less easily detected than a hastily performed job. The floor molding or skirting should be removed before commencing work, as the layout and type of board used for the floor will be clearly visible, and there will be less risk of split or damaged boards.

Also remember the weight of objects to be hidden below flooring if the floor is covering a ceiling upon which the stash is to rest. Heavy objects should be packed in wide, long containers or on similarly shaped bases. This helps to spread the weight over a greater area and decreases the risk of the goods falling straight through the plaster.

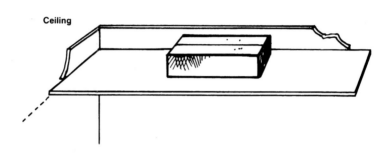

Board used to spread weight of object

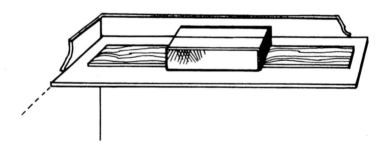

False ceilings, taking the form of anything from plasti-glass panels to ornate wooden designs, lend themselves nicely to the stashing of goods. Sometimes called suspended ceilings, they are affixed to strips or hangers that have been attached to the original ceiling. Sometimes lighting tubes are fitted above these ceilings, and if this is the case a hide within a hide is easily achieved. If no such ceiling exists in your target building, the quickest way of constructing one is as follows.

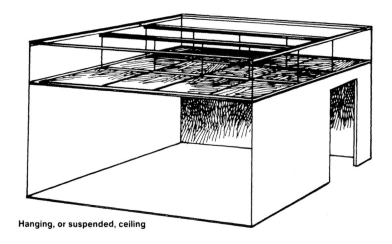

Hanging, or suspended, ceiling

Obtain a quantity of narrow, lath strips of sufficient length to pattern the ceiling as shown below. Next your chosen material (plasti-glass, wood board, tiling, or what-

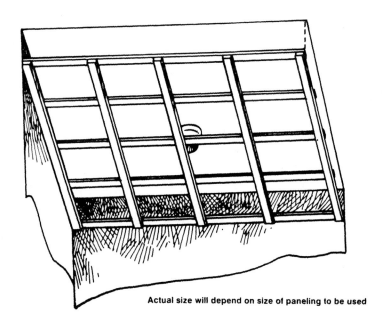

Actual size will depend on size of paneling to be used

ever) is attached to the strips by screws or adhesive. Clips which will secure most materials safely can also be found at hardware stores. These can take many different forms, but the guy in the store will assist you if you explain what you are doing (more or less!).

A couple of panels in place

The area of the stash is selected so as to be accessible but not obvious—not under the only tile or board that is removable for access to lighting, for example. If simple wall board covering is used (or plasterboard, which is used for ceiling construction and repair anyway) the whole thing can be painted or papered or tiled as desired when finished to give the impression of an original ceiling. Don't forget to allow for the lighting wire during construction.

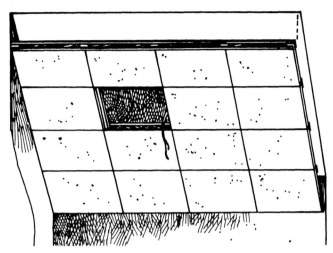

Center panel left until lighting is extended

By sensibly selecting the type of light fitting to be mounted when the ceiling is completed, the screws that will release a board can be hidden behind the light unit itself. The fixing screws for the two strip-light units can also hold the ceiling board door in position. The ceiling should be tiled to create a visually confusing pattern which makes locating any likely join or hinge area difficult.

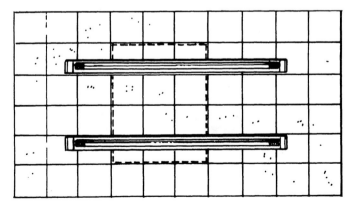

Looking up

There are also a few places where items may be hidden that require no construction at all. The most obvious of these is the good old mail service. One commonly used method of "losing" items, documents and so on, is to simply post the package to yourself or to a safe address from where it will in turn be sent back to you. You then send it back, and so on. This technique ensures that the item is never in anyone's possession for more than an hour or so at the most, but it also presupposes that the contents of the package are not going to attract undue attention at the mail offices.

As a cover, enclose some sort of letter to the effect that the sender of the package is in fact sending the package to you without your prior knowledge. There are many variations that will do the trick, and it gives just that bit more security if the package is intercepted or found in your possession. Needless to say, the information (if any) regarding the sender should be fictitious and the package sent from an office or via a box that is outside of your normal area of residence.

Another expedient method of losing an item when things are getting hot is to drop the package into a mail box. The chances of the box being stolen are pretty remote, and the only factor to take care of is that you are ready and waiting when the mailman comes to empty the box. This method is regularly used to store small packages overnight, when there is no mail pick-up. In the morning, when the mail van arrives to empty the box, one simply approaches the mailman and explains how you accidentally posted the wrong item. Make sure that you can identify the package easily, and have it appear obvious that the package could not have been actually intended for posting as it has no stamps, address, and so on. You would be surprised how many people post their wallet or purse in error.

If you are stuck for a hide at your country retreat area,

and if you like to do things in style, the following hide is definitely for you. We will assume that you have access to one or more substantially sized trees in the area of your retreat, and that there are no prying eyes to watch your activities.

Select a tree with as large a diameter as possible while still allowing you to manhandle it. The tree should also be of the below ground type, that is, its roots, and also the roots of similar trees in the area, should be completely covered and not showing above the surface. The first step is to cut down the tree as near to ground level as possible and remove the remaining root stump.

Next, a length of metal or concrete pipe is sunk into the ground at the spot where the tree stood. The top of the pipe should be several inches below the ground surface, as shown below. The pipe should be of sufficient diameter

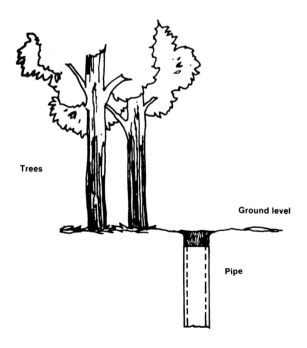

to receive the base end of the tree, and should be of sufficient length to resist any levering effect that the tree, once inserted into the pipe, is likely to create when swaying. The specific length and diameter of the pipe will be determined by the size of the tree.

The next stage is to bore out a cavity from the base of the tree large enough to conceal the items in question. Care must be taken that the cavity does not exceed commonsense limits; that is to say that enough width must be left in the shell of the base to provide support. A few tests showed that at least a quarter of the original diameter should be left intact to provide the required support. This still gives more than adequate space in all but the skinniest of trees. With the items secured, and water-protected if required, the tree is replanted into its

Base of tree shown hollowed out

pipe-holder. The surrounding earth is used along with general debris to finish the job and conceal any trace of the pipe base. This is a fantastic hide if used on one or two trees amongst many. It will take many weeks for the tree to show sign of distress.

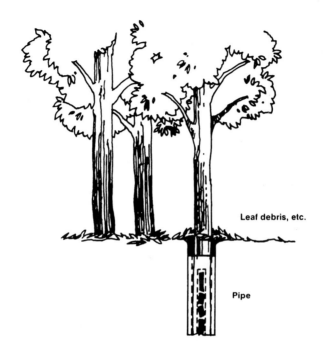

Leaf debris, etc.

Pipe

It is also possible to use a sort of double bluff technique to get away with hiding persons in the most unlikely, yet obvious places around the home. People were amazed recently when the British press reported on the capture, by police, of a guy who had been on the run for several months. He was not wanted for any serious crime, but he was convinced that the punishment for his offenses would be severe. Apparently he stumbled on his hiding place by accident. He had jumped bail and was sweating it out at home. British police being what they are, they considered it unlikely that he would be silly enough to go straight home, so they left quite a gap between his jumping bail and their visit to his home.

This apparent lack of interest spurred our friendly bail-jumper's confidence, and after a while he began to carry on with his life more or less as normal. He didn't risk leaving the house, and, being motivated by fear rather than cunning intent, he made no plans to skip town. The first visit by the police in search of our friend was apparently provoked by a report that he had been seen in the local pub, but this was later proved to be an excuse for bothering the guy's wife.

Now, the knock at the door which heralded the arrival of the boys in blue happened to coincide with our friend's attempts to repair a faulty washing machine in the kitchen of his home. Most of the innards of the machine had been removed and taken to the workshop in the yard for overhaul, leaving a few minor pump parts in the otherwise hollow machine, and it was to these parts that his attention was turned. In a moment of panic (that's his story anyway) he clambered into the machine, which was of the front loading type, pulling a few items of washing over him to create the illusion to onlookers that the machine was ready for use.

In due course the police entered the house, and what is reported to have been a thorough search of the property took place. None of the officers thought to examine the washer closely, and this lack of enthusiasm or skill was repeated on several other occasions during searches over the following year. Eventually a nosy neighbor spotted our friend in the garden and called the police, who arrived and caught him off guard. It should be said that he was in fact fed up with his secret existence, and he was actually pleased to get the affair over with.

The moral of the story (in fact it contains a few!) is clear, and it got me thinking about similar places that with a little preparation would serve as hiding places unlikely to be even considered by the average policeman or other searchers. I found that apart from the washing machine (with the rotating drum removed) there were several other items that worked well. I am keeping a couple of them to myself, just in case, but here are a few possibilities that should be of use.

Always spend some time preparing the selected hide, as the effort will be more than rewarded if you get away with it. Also bear in mind that the success of this type of hide relies on the fact that the searcher is looking for people, and people are not generally expected to be found wedged inside washing machines. There is no logical link in the mind of the searcher between the size, shape, and weight of the person for whom he is searching and small or confined areas usually associated with other purposes than containment of humans. If the searcher is looking for goods as well as personnel, or if he is just *looking,* this effect is reduced if not totally lost.

The large type of fitted bedroom closet containing wardrobe, drawers, and overhead units, as shown, is ideal

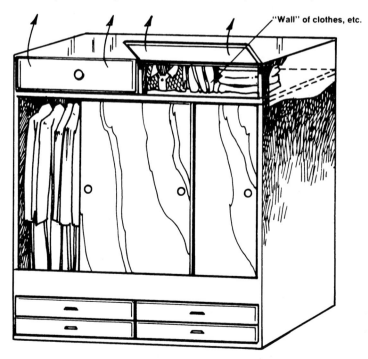

"Wall" of clothes, etc.

for hiding personnel. Use the top units and ensure that an adequate supply of clothes or whatever is kept there to provide the camouflage. In the majority of searches for persons, the large wardrobe itself will be opened but the top unit will be ignored or at worst examined only in a cursory fashion.

The drawers themselves, if cunningly altered, will do just as well. Simply remove the drawers and remove enough of their length to enable you to secrete yourself behind them and replace them. As long as the drawers slide out a few inches, they will serve the purpose, but in most modern units there is adequate space for about six inches to be removed from the back of the drawers, enabling a person to hide without giving the game away. Always have the drawers full of "rubbish," and leave one of them partially open so that any searcher can readily see that a human being could not possibly be hidden within. Concealment, not comfort, is the name of the game.

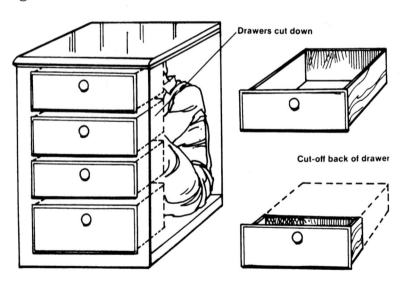

Drawers cut down

Cut-off back of drawer

Person hidden behind converted drawers

The bases of modern divan beds are easily doctored by removing the bottom covering of material. This is often simply stapled on. Cut away enough of the internal padding to take your shape, attaching velcro strips or any other convenient form of fastening to allow you to replace the base once you are hidden within. Access may also be gained via any drawers which may be fitted to the bed.

Base view of divan

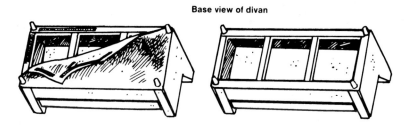

Base shown with cover removed to reveal strengthening braces; these easily support a man's weight.

Large rack music systems can also be prepared to conceal a fair-sized person. The type of system I experimented with was a large but commonly available J.V.C. set-up. Of course, it is only the size of the actual unit that matters, not the equipment within. Indeed, as the conversion requires the butchering of most of the equipment, the items will probably be selected for their low value. Don't underdo it though, as a flash looking unit which houses very cheap and nasty audio gear might attract interest. The audio equipment that is to be housed in the unit is disassembled until only a fascia affair is left, as shown. The front of the items when placed in the unit gives the impression that it is all above board. The stack of records at the bottom are cut down in a similar fashion to create the same illusion. There is no need, obviously, to butcher the record deck, as this sits atop the unit as shown. The beauty of the cabinet I used was that it also had a lock on the front door to deter nosy searchers from looking to see if you have their favorite record.

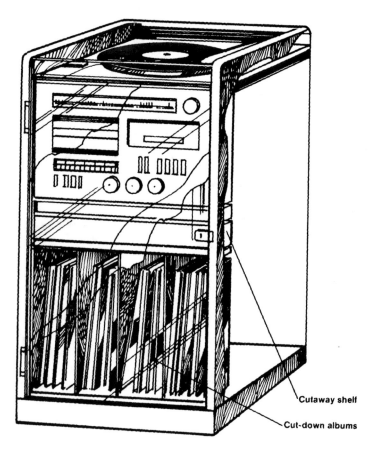

Cutaway shelf

Cut-down albums

Front or side view of system gives impression of normalcy.

Cut-down album cover

Cut-down tape

It is amazing just how small a space the human body can be fitted into. Discomfort is to be expected of course, but so what? If you evade the searchers, you will remember that cramped neck fondly for years to come. Better start watching your weight, just in case!

3. SECRET SAFE SPACES FOR PERSONNEL

Anyone WHO HAS LIVED THROUGH A WAR IN their home country or who can imagine the terror of people subjected to raids on their homes will appreciate the value of a hiding place large enough to secrete a person or even a family. For years, talk of building bomb shelters against radioactive fallout has been in vogue. Considering the anarchy that could occur after a holocaust of almost any kind or even the extent and seriousness of terrorism these days, building a secret, safe place that is within reach of the house or office becomes plausible.

A selection of simple tools is required to make these structures, but no knowledge of carpentry is needed. The diagrams and notes are given as guidelines only, and it is taken for granted that you will adapt and improvise them, as and when required. The bottom line is that the finished structure appears normal, is sound, and will withstand fairly thorough scrutiny. It is not necessary that the finished designs meet local building regulations!

The first of these designs is for a basic hidden room. The design possibilities are endless, but a few rules should be remembered.

- Be realistic about the size of the room. If someone enters the blind—the room within which is the hidden room—

and it measures only five by two feet, has no electric power outlets, furniture, or windows and sports a huge, freshly decorated wall, they might get a bit suspicious!

- Pay attention to detail if the room is to fool any but the most stupid examiners. If windows are visible from the outside of the building, but no corresponding room seems to exist. . . !
- Make sure that some method of determining what is going on outside the room exists. There is not a lot of use having a hidden room if you are unable to tell when whoever you are hiding from has gone and it is safe to leave! Of course, the room may not be for people, in which case the last point is not so important. However, you will not want to exit the room after a hard day's counterfeiting and walk into the arms of a visiting policeman.

For a simple nonroom where the required space is not too great, simply fencing off a section of an existing room will suffice. Remember the points mentioned earlier, and measure up.

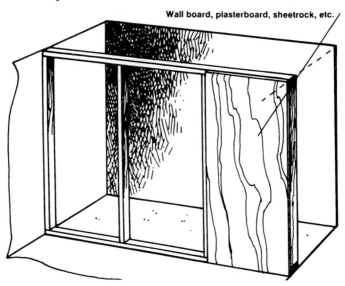

Wall board, plasterboard, sheetrock, etc.

You will need either sufficient bricks and mortar (if the false wall is supposed to be an outside wall) or sufficient lengths of timber to construct the frame shown below (if you are merely moving the location of a dividing wall). You will also require some wall boards, thin hardboard, or the like.

The frame is fixed in place as above, and the false wall attached. When fitting the final section of wall, remember to make some provision for entering and exiting the room. This could take the form of a section of spongy foam rubber which is fitted to the top and bottom of the piece of wallboard and the frame. The screws are tightened home, compressing the spongy rubber. When the screws are loosened, however, the rubber springs back into shape, pushing the board clear of the frame and the surrounding boards. This method of release makes it unnecessary to have anything protruding from the board (which, after all, is supposed to be a wall, not a door). It may be found that when the screws are loosened the boards will fall away from the frame naturally. On occasion, however, they stick to the frame, especially if they have not been undone for some time. As the whole thing is perfectly

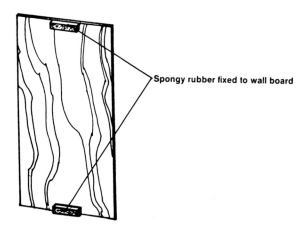

Spongy rubber fixed to wall board

flush fitted, a stuck board would necessitate the insertion of a screwdriver or other tool to lever the board away from the frame. The resulting scratch could give the game away.

When wall boards (the store-bought, imitation wood or wood veneer boards) are used, it will not be necessary to disguise the screw heads. When used in normal situations, these boards are usually fastened to firring strips that have been attached to the wall, and the screws are visible. If plain boards are used, wallpaper or some other wall covering should be used to disguise them. In order that access can be obtained quickly, while still giving no clue that the wall is a dummy, wallpaper should be applied using artist's glue, or rubber cement, instead of wallpaper paste. This type of glue is sprayed on from an aerosol can. The wallpaper will be held firmly in place but can be easily peeled back to reveal the screws. The glue will enable the paper to be stuck down and peeled back countless times without losing its adhesive qualities.

To facilitate the closing of the door from the inside without leaving any telltale traces on the outside, use the following method.

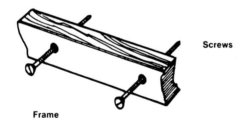

Screws

Frame

In the section of frame that is to hold the door, drill out holes in the places where the screws will enter. Use oversize (very long) screws that protrude through the frame into the room by several inches. Next, affix a piece of wood to the back of the frame so that with *no* pressure from the outside on the board the screw does not quite reach the piece of backing wood, but *with* pressure from the outside applied to the board the screw makes contact and can be tightened normally. Wood glue is useful for fixing the backing block to the frame, as it provides enough adhesion to enable the screws to be driven in from the outside, yet will allow the block to be knocked off the frame again with little force. It is important that the screw

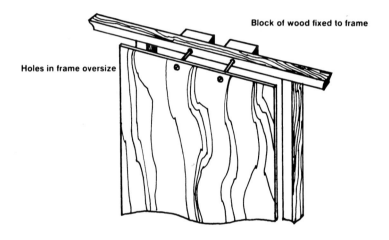

Block of wood fixed to frame

Holes in frame oversize

is of such a size (diameter) that it will not fall out of the wall board when it is unfastened, but rather unscrews from the piece of backing wood. This is to prevent the wallpaper (if used) from being seen in a peeled back condition by anyone entering the real room while the false room is in use. If the screw keeps falling out or is loose, affix a suitably sized spring collar (available from hardware stores) to the inside of the board where the screw passes through. With this fitted, the screw can be turned, but it will not screw out of the wall board.

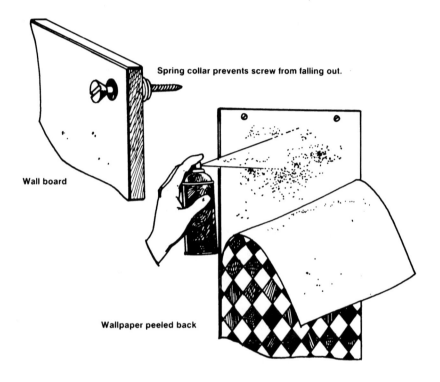

Spring collar prevents screw from falling out.

Wall board

Wallpaper peeled back

When using the room, unfasten the door and then replace the wallpaper over the screws before entering. To lock the door from the inside, remove the backing block from the frame and screw it home onto the screw. This will pull the wall board back into place, leaving no trace of the activity within.

For added security, the inside of the wall boards can be covered with a sandwich of insulation. Automobile insulating felt is also suitable. The walls of the room can be covered with this material as well, as its effect is to deaden the echoing sound of the room should the wall boards be tapped during a search. It makes the boards themselves sound and feel more substantial as well.

A cheap and simple bug is by far the best means of determining whether the outside room is safe when you are on the inside. Available almost everywhere, these small electronic transmitters can be tuned into on normal domestic radios. FM is most common, usually around 80 to 100 Mhz. They are sensitive. Hide the bug in the outside room and monitor on headphones or an earpiece.

As for the use of a concrete or brick wall, short of bricking yourself in, or getting someone on the outside to do it, there is no way that a foolproof hidden room can be constructed with an undetectable method of entry and exit. Unless . . . Obviously a false wall made from brick or the like cannot have the entrance actually in it. However, if we combine two likely hides as follows, we get the desired effect. The selected blind should be checked for adequate underfloor space before commencing. Simply pull up a floor board and see if it is possible for you or the largest person likely to use the hide to crawl underneath it. It may be found, depending on location, that there is enough space under the floor itself for your purposes. If this is the case, just prepare the door according to the directions below. More often than not, however, there will be enough room to crawl beneath the floor, but little else. This is perfect for our needs.

The next thing to do is pace out the rough position that the hidden room is to take and lift another floor board. Now check that it is possible to crawl from one place to the other. If it is, go ahead and build your wall. For obvious reasons, make sure that any large objects to be used in the room are placed in position before the wall is built. Decorate the wall to fit in with the rest of the room and then turn your attention to the door. The boards that you need to remove in order to get under the floor should be placed onto a hardboard backing and

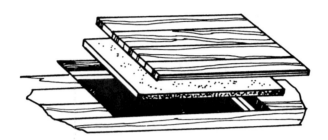

secured with high powered adhesive. The end product will be a trap door affair, as shown above. The underfloor beams should be fashioned so that they will receive the door with a tight-fitting, positive action; no giveaway lumps or bulges should be visible when any floor covering is replaced. (See the end of this section.) You will probably get away with using a small handsaw, hammer, and chisel for the cutting and shaping work.

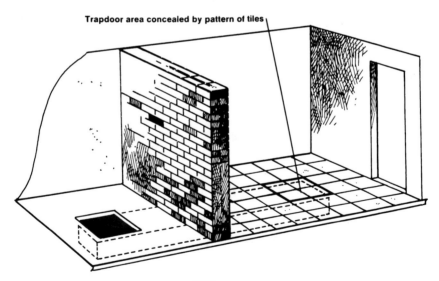

Trapdoor area concealed by pattern of tiles

Hidden room

And that's about it. One crawls from the door under the floor and up into the hidden room. Once again, make sure that adequate outside monitoring facilities are installed. To emphasize the need for such facilities, I must make a quick reference to some of the other publications covering this topic that are on the market. While useful for some applications, many of these publications explain how, for example, a hidden room may be constructed. They detail the actual building of a wall, and suggest methods of entry that a blind three-year-old could find. Alternatively, they give excellent entrance/exit methods, but neglect to mention that they cannot be operated from the inside. Now, that's fine if the room is to be used for nonhuman contents. If anyone pops in while the room is in use, you simply close the door, and any search will turn nothing up. Where this is the case, very primitive entry and exit designs and camouflage techniques can be used with a degree of success. However, as for the comments in many such books that, "such and such method is not worth the trouble," I can only assume that if "such and such is not worth the trouble," then the goods, people or whatever you might intend to hide are not worth much either! Time and trouble will repay you a hundredfold; always remember that.

A few notes about camouflage are in order here. When using the underfloor entry method, always select a floor covering that lends itself naturally to visual confusion. That means the surface pattern or design of the covering is *not* a plain, single colored, single shaded type, such as a plain one-piece carpet or piece of linoleum. *Always,* where possible and when the job warrants it, use either carpet tiles or parquet floor coverings. By using tiling or parquet covering, the door area is concealed naturally, as shown.

It is impossible to tunnel under an uncut carpet in order to reach the door without loosening the carpet so obviously that anyone entering the room after you will notice immediately what is going on, and coming up with a method for relaying the carpet once you have passed beneath it is beyond me. Any cut-out made in a plain, one-piece carpet to cover the trapdoor would be apparent.

Visually confusing patterns will effectively conceal trapdoor location.

You could fix a rug to the top of the door for camouflage, but even then, although the room would appear normal on casual examination, an attempt to move the rug would probably be made during a search. More about eye confusion techniques later.

There is an even simpler way of constructing a secret room, requiring much less effort. This is the preferred technique when the layout of the building permits. You are effectively going to make an existing room disappear.

The first step is the obvious one of removing doors and any door trim. The doorway is filled in with a combination of plasterboard, plaster and insulation material, leaving sufficient room, of course, for you to enter and leave with whatever you may desire. Use the minimum space that will do. Make or buy a shelf assembly to serve as your door. One of the back panels of the unit is doctored (using any of the techniques shown herein), and away you go. The points to remember are that if the room is to be used for personnel, some method of securing the door from the inside without leaving telltale signs on the outside must be devised. A possibility is shown below.

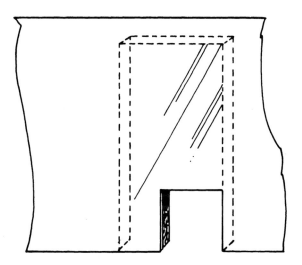

Old door location covered by plasterboard, with inside of board covered with insulation to lessen echoing effect

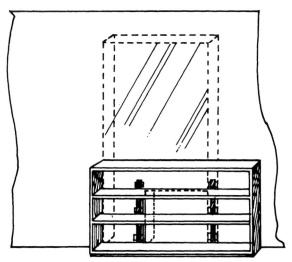

The back panel and shelves are held in place with powerful magnets which mate with metal strips on the frame area of the room entrance. To remove the panel simply grasp the shelf and pull. A handle is attached to the room side of the panel so that it may be placed in position from the inside. A couple of screws should also be used from the inside of the room to lock the panel into the rest of the shelf unit.

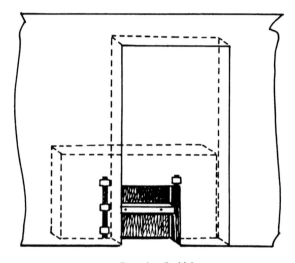

Rear view (inside)

Ornaments, books, or the like should be left on the shelves, and it is important to select these carefully, or custom-build the shelf unit around selected articles so that the false shelf and panel can be lifted in and out without disturbing them. Small pieces of sticky pad can be used to secure items to the shelf. Your level of construction will depend on what degree of search, if any, you anticipate.

Where circumstances permit and the effort involved is justified, excellent hides can be constructed in the garden or other outside areas.

Numerous plans for underground shelter constructions can be found in most military surplus stores. These are easily modified to suit specific requirements. Remember, of course, to pay particular attention to the disguise and camouflage aspects of the design. A simple underground hide can be constructed as follows, the only materials required being several two-by-fours, some plywood sections, and a quantity of concrete or cement.

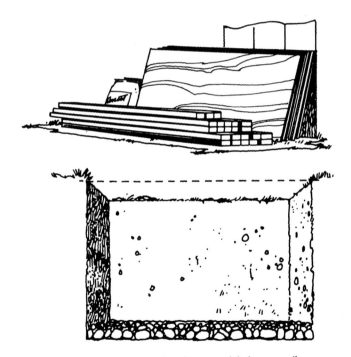

Base of hide lined with rocks removed during excavation

The first stage of the operation is obviously to measure out the area of the ground to be used and dig out to the desired depth. Any rocks that you uncover during the excavation should be retained, as they will come in handy as foundation hardcore for the base of the structure. When the required size is obtained, layer the base of the excavation with the largest rocks at the bottom and any small gravel forming the final top layer as shown above. The cement mix is now poured over the rock base, and voila, you have a floor. If considered necessary, drainage can be facilitated by inserting a suitably sized pole through the cement and the rock base into the earth below. This pole is removed just before the cement hardens completely as shown below. The floor may also be sloped slightly to improve run off capabilities.

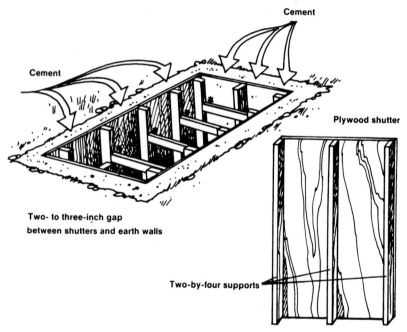

Cement

Cement

Plywood shutter

Two- to three-inch gap
between shutters and earth walls

Two-by-four supports

The simplest method for constructing the walls and roof area is to make up a series of shutters, as shown, which are used to line the wall area of the dugout. The two-by-fours support the plywood frame, and the whole assembly is secured using two-by-four braces (shown above). The cement is poured into the framework and

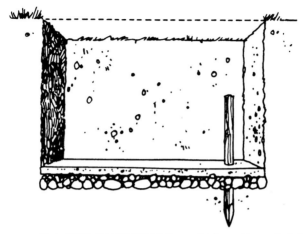

Base of hide, showing cement floor and pole used to create drain

left for at least a couple of days to dry thoroughly. Reinforcing bars made from salvaged steel can be used if desired, but the finished structure will be strong enough for most uses. A thin film of linseed oil applied to the inside of the plywood framework before final assembly will provide for easier removal when the cement is dry.

Although shutters can be constructed in a similar fashion to make the roof, casting off-site is just as simple by using sheets of corrugated iron covered with polythene plastic, as shown. The corrugated iron sheets lend themselves well to use as molds, as the ridges can be used to secure any reinforcing bars that may be used. A simple brick wall can also be used to prevent the cement from running off before it begins to harden and to give the casting extra depth. Once set, simply put the roof sections in place, paving-slab fashion.

The roof sections are cast slightly oversize to provide a good fit when placed on the concrete wall and to enable good camouflage to be effected by using the surrounding earth. It should be noted that the hide itself must be sunk

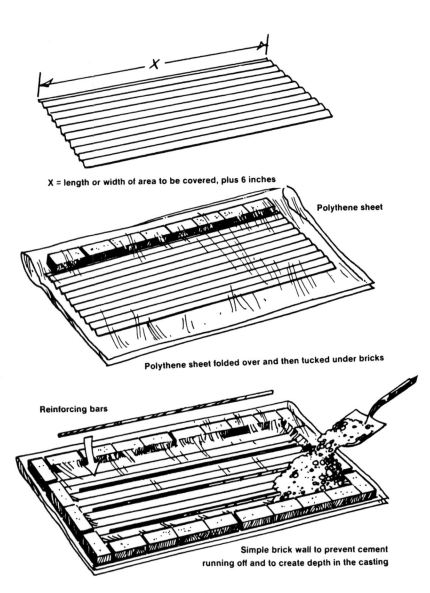

X = length or width of area to be covered, plus 6 inches

Polythene sheet

Polythene sheet folded over and then tucked under bricks

Reinforcing bars

Simple brick wall to prevent cement
running off and to create depth in the casting

The iron sheet is lined with polythene and the wall built around it. The bricks also secure
the polythene during pouring. Half the mix is poured in, and before it is completely hard
the bars are inserted. The remainder of the mix is then added.

slightly below ground level to allow for the fitting of the roof without creating a mound. The finished roof should be almost flush with the surrounding ground. The entrance is made by casting an undersize roof section and the doorway camouflaged by any number of possible methods according to the location of the hide. One possibility is to hide the shelter beneath some sort of garden patio constructed from paving slabs; entry is effected by simply lifting your chosen door slab.

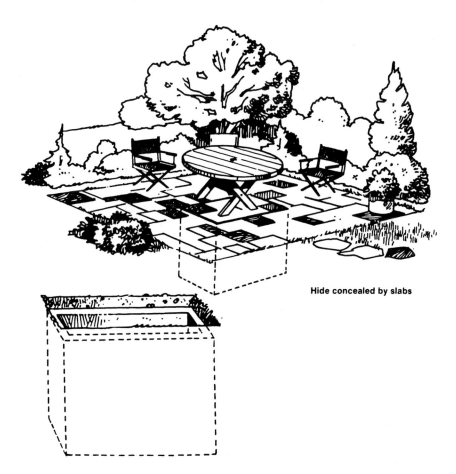

Hide concealed by slabs

A few other unorthodox techniques that can be employed in the construction of concrete underground hides are given below. With a little ingenuity, a lot of time and expense can be saved when undertaking such projects.

A very useful method for making preformed wall or roof units from cement or for casting on-site is the use of airbeds or plastic rafts like the ones used on the beach.

The existing valve assembly is removed and a larger access port affixed using super glue or vinyl repair glue. These products are obtainable from hardware outlets and swimming pool supply shops.

If an on-site casting is requiring, the airbeds are affixed in place, loosely at first, and the cement mixture pumped inside. The old-fashioned type of stirrup, or foot, pump can be used for this with excellent results. As the beds fill with cement and begin to take shape the fixing braces are readjusted to maintain a secure fitting in the required position.

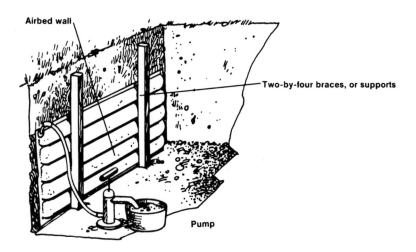

Airbed wall

Two-by-four braces, or supports

Pump

While testing this method, I found that air pockets formed within the bed as the cement was pumped in.

These are easily removed by piercing the rubber with a small pin or nail. The air and some water will be forced out, but the cement, as it hardens, prevents the hole widening unduly and cement being lost. Once the cement hardens the rubber mold can be peeled off or left in place for a very professional-looking finish.

The inner tubes of large truck tires can be used in a similar fashion to create a wide variety of useful castings, the most obvious of these being roof support pillars for underground connecting tunnels. It is worth

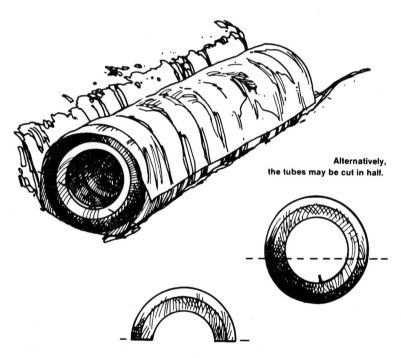

Alternatively, the tubes may be cut in half.

Once set, the tubes may be used as a one-piece unit, in which case the lower half is buried.

noting that if a long term of use is anticipated from an underground cement-based structure, more care should be paid to the use of reinforcing materials. Metal bars, unless completely rust-free and protected by suitable paint, will deteriorate within the cement after a time, and gases given off due to chemical reaction will split the cement. Air pockets will also have a detrimental effect on the long-term safety of cement structures. These points are really only valid if you intend to use an underground hide for personnel over prolonged periods when safety will be of paramount importance.

An ornamental pool is another possibility. The ground surrounding the hide is adjusted so that the pool body (of the preformed plastic type) can be dropped into the earth covering the door of the hide.

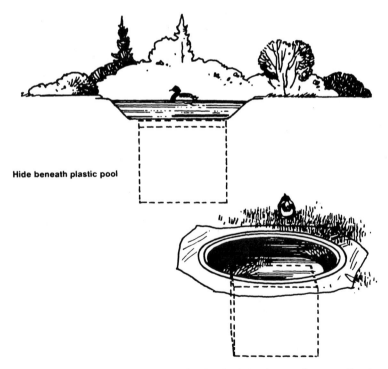

Hide beneath plastic pool

Side view of pool, showing rim that rests on earth surrounding door

Alternatively, the area could be turfed over, as shown. An outbuilding could be built over the top of the underground hide and flooring used to effect the disguise.

Tray containing turf lifts in and out.

A sheet of suitable material is used to cover the door and turf affixed so that the lid and turf can be removed as one.

Or for a really flash hide, a small garden pool could be constructed over the top of the underground hide, access only being obtainable by draining the pool and removing the butyl rubber base, which itself would give access to the door panel (this could be a paving slab). The possibilities are endless, but this should have given you a few ideas.

If you don't want to go to the length of using cement, a very useful underground hide can be made in a similar fashion to that shown previously but with corrugated iron sheets used in place of the cement. Once the dugout is made, several lengths of angle-iron, wooden stakes, or other suitable objects should be affixed along the walls

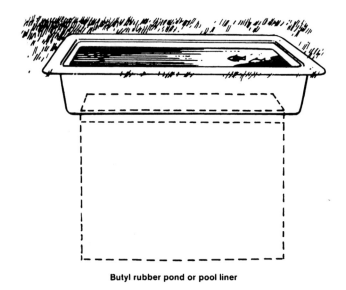

Butyl rubber pond or pool liner

of the dugout as shown below. The sheets of corrugated iron are attached to these "fence-posts" with nails, screws, or the like until a metal wall is completed. Next, to the

Corrugated iron

top of the "fence-posts," attach more sheets of the corrugated iron until you have a roof. Depending on size of the dugout, it may be necessary to fix support braces beneath the roof, as shown.

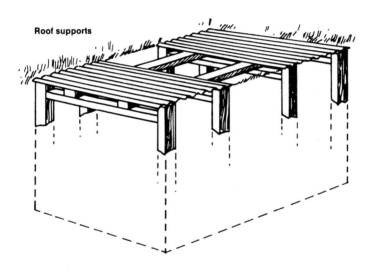

Roof supports

A more elaborate system of roof support beams can be employed which will give the structure considerably more rigidity. Turfing is the best form of camouflage for such a hide, with the door taking the form of a small bush which is actually planted in a tub and then planted atop the door area. You will get a better idea of what I mean here from the diagram.

Satisfactory underground hides can also be constructed using sand bags as walls, military fashion, and a sheet of strong Kippex material can be used as a roof in many instances with great effect. Kippex is a brand name of a type of manmade material used in the manufacture of tenting. It is very strong if tightly sprung and makes for superb expedient hides.

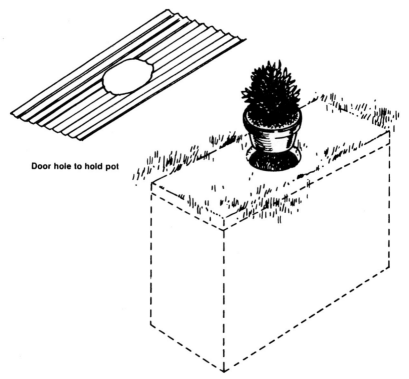

Door hole to hold pot

Soil completely covers pot so that only the bush is visible.

A length of pipe of the type used in sewer construction and often left lying around unattended on building sites can be put to good use in the field of hide construction. Simply sinking the pipe vertically in your yard will make a great hide. If you look carefully you will probably be able to find a suitably sized manhole cover that will make the finished thing that bit more professional. Were such a technique used, it would be a simple matter to install a stop plate of wood halfway down the pipe to cover the goods or person so that the top half could be filled with grungy water deterring most would-be searchers and creating the illusion of a genuine in-use pipe.

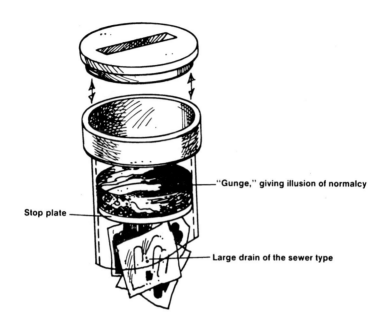

"Gunge," giving illusion of normalcy

Stop plate

Large drain of the sewer type

The use of a two-way mirror to monitor what is going on outside a hidden room from within is a well-known practice. It may be that you are to undertake some sort of surveillance operation where a hidden camera is to be used, or maybe you just want a quick and simple method of checking that the outside area of the hidden room is clear before you make your exit. Once again, the possible uses are endless, but such mirrors are often expensive to purchase, especially if you require a custom-built one to suit a specific purpose. With a little work, however, you can make your own two-way mirrors cheaply and easily. As the construction of these two-way mirrors requires the use of chemicals, be sure to take normal precautions including the wearing of gloves and, if available, protective glasses.

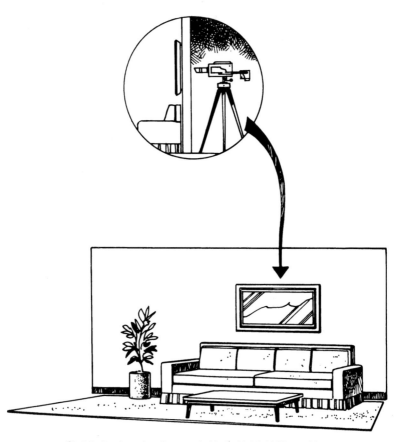

Sketch showing mirror in room, behind which is hidden a video camera

Normal window glass is used, and the first step is to ensure that the selected piece is chemically clean. This is best achieved by bathing the glass in a sugar soap solution, or by swabbing with dilute acid. Sugar soap is a chemical product used by decorators. It contains no soap as such, and soap should never be used in an attempt to clean the glass. After either of these treatments wash down the glass with clean water. Leave the glass, supported at only its edges, to dry naturally. During this time you can prepare the chemicals needed as follows.

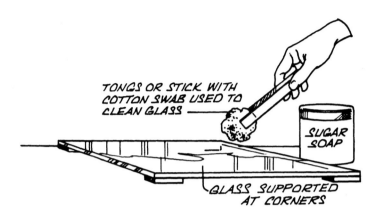

First, obtain three glass containers; jam jars will do nicely. Mark the jars 1, 2, and 3 to avoid confusion later. Into the first jar, pour 300 mls of distilled water and to this add 28 gs of silver nitrate. Stir well.

Into the second jar, pour 30 mls of the solution from jar one.

The next stage is to add with an eye dropper small quantities of aqua ammonia (10 percent strength is enough) to the solution in jar one. As the aqua ammonia is added the solution will turn brown but then clear again as the solution is stirred. Continue adding the ammonia until the solution only just clears, or is just on the verge of remaining brown. At this stage the mix is correct.

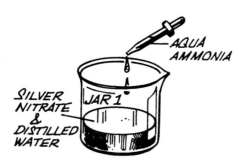

The solution for jar three is made *exactly* as follows. Pour 300 mls of distilled water into the jar and then slowly add, in small amounts, 28 gs of caustic potash. A degree of heat is generated as the chemicals mix, and the resulting solution must be allowed to cool before continuing with the process, which is simply to add the contents of jar three to those of jar one. Stir the solution, and add small quantities of aqua ammonia until the solution is neither fully clouded nor completely brown.

Next add the solution in jar two to that in jar one. The mixture will now turn dark brown again. The final stage in the preparation of the mixture is to add 15 gs of common glucose to 300 mls of distilled water. Stir well and add this to jar one. This mix is the final working solution. The glass to be used is supported at its edges, and a shelf or wall of melted wax or putty affixed around

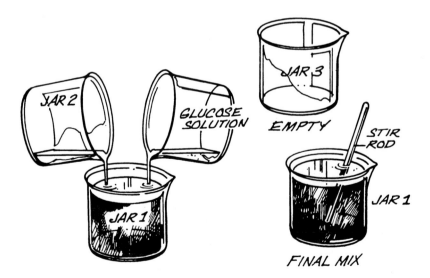

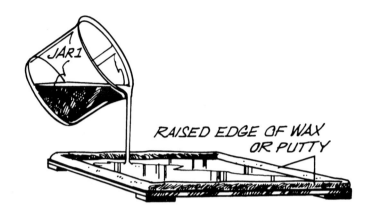

RAISED EDGE OF WAX
OR PUTTY

the upper edge, as shown above. The solution in jar one is poured over the glass until the surface is thinly but uniformly covered.

Leave the glass for about twenty-five minutes to allow the process to take effect. At intervals of a few minutes, look from underneath the glass to see that a mirror surface is forming. At the same time, check that some item placed beneath the glass is visible from above. Once this stage is reached, pour off any excess solution and rinse the glass under running water. Allow it to dry naturally. A thin coat of clear varnish or plastic seal can be applied to the treated (see-through side) of the glass for added protection. In position, the effect is heightened if the mirror-side area is well lit and the see-through side (hidden room) is somewhat darker.

The technique for cutting glass, or tiles for that matter, is given below. Using this method saves on time and also on glass! Place the glass on a level surface padded with rags or newspaper and mark the dimensions to be cut using a pencil or felt-tip pen. Place a straight edged tool across the marks and score the surface with one smooth

stroke of the glass cutter. Hold the cutter as shown above. Don't be tempted to make another score with the cutter, as this damages the cutting wheel.

Next place the glass over the ruler (or other straight edge) as shown and press down on both sides, snapping the glass cleanly in two. If patterned glass is used, the score mark is of course made on the smooth side.

A common type of mirror fixing is shown below, and the illustration alongside shows a possible location for a two-way mirror, in the hallway of a home where a hidden camera could be used to record the comings and goings of visitors, invited or otherwise! You'd be surprised how many people unconsciously adjust their clothing or hair in front of a mirror, making for a good picture if a hidden camera is in use.

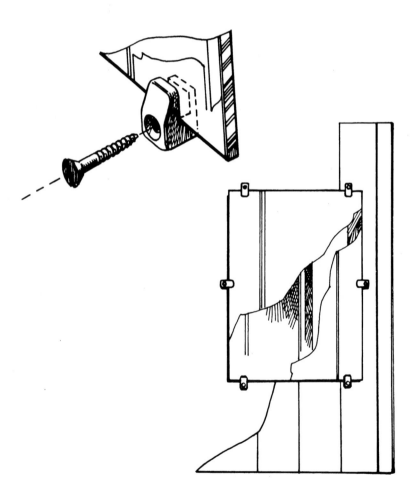

Always remember when using velcro or magnetic strip and metal fastening techniques that for a flush, and therefore unnoticeable, fit the fastening material should be recessed as shown below. Simply attaching the fastening material to one or both surfaces will result in the joint being easily detectable. Magnetic fastening techniques are to be preferred as their use facilitates rapid removal and placement of the door without the need for any attachments whatsoever. Simply apply a more powerful magnet than that being used as the fastener. Double-layer cooking foil tacked into the recess with magnetic strip or several single magnets attached to the door inner is one method of fixing.

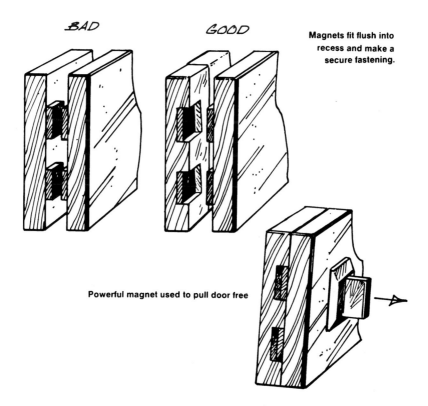

BAD

GOOD

Magnets fit flush into recess and make a secure fastening.

Powerful magnet used to pull door free

Another very useful form of fixing two-way mirrors in place is to use a spring-loaded magnetic catch, as shown below. This type of catch is available from many hardware outlets, and is also used on many home hi-fi systems.

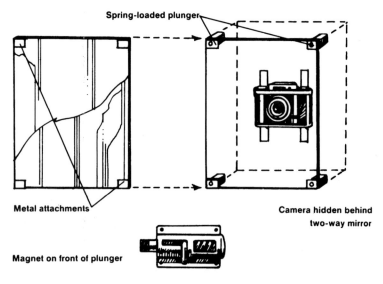

Spring-loaded plunger

Metal attachments

Magnet on front of plunger

Camera hidden behind two-way mirror

Spring-loaded plunger assembly

As the spring-loaded plunger is depressed, a latch at the rear of the plunger engages with a cut-out. The plunger remains locked rearward, and the door is held tight against the front of the plunger by a small but powerful magnet. To open the door, the door itself is pushed from the front, which releases the pawl on the plunger, pushing it outward; the door flies open. The metal attachments required on a section of two-way mirror are easily disguised as normal wall fittings or embellishments. Should it be necessary to close the door from within, a strong, glass cutter's sucker pad can be used, as illustrated in the diagram on the next page.

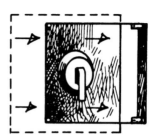

Mirror turned at an angle and passed through opening into room, then pulled back against the spring fasteners

Plunger used to handle mirror from behind

4. AWAY-FROM-HOME HIDES

Patrons of hotels and motels are truly sitting ducks for burglars no matter how good security may seem. You may have considerable amounts of cash or other valuables with you that you have no desire to have taken from you by the first down-and-out with a gun that happens to collar you. And yet you may have no desire to draw attention to your possessions by opting for the hotel safe; many rip-offs go down after a watch has been made of persons depositing valuables in hotel safes during their stay. They reclaim the goods, leave the hotel, and head for the car park, and—well, chances are they never make it.

Here are a few stashes that apply not only to home base, but also to hotel, motel or any temporary quarters.

Next time you have occasion to stay in a motel, have a look for a wall-mounted radio speaker. Most hotels mount these so that they cannot be easily stolen by visitors, yet it is still possible to get to the inside of the unit for repair. If the front of the speaker appears to be covered completely with acoustic foam, have a quick tug at one corner; usually it will peel off to reveal four or more screws. Undo these and you will be able to get at the inside.

The bathroom has to be the first choice for this type of hide. Not only are bathrooms areas in which people under normal circumstances spend little time, or visit infrequently, but a visit to the bathroom takes little justification. "Do you mind if I use your attic?" just doesn't ring true, does it? However, several minutes can be spent in friends' bathrooms without arousing the slightest suspicion. Hotel bathrooms are cleaned (sometimes) by disinterested people, and the chances of any radical difference in the design or layout of the target bathroom between the time you make the stash and the time you return to collect is highly unlikely.

Paneling, especially that around the bath itself, is easily removed with a small screwdriver, and it is usually possible to obtain sufficient access by removing only a

Most panels are unscrewed easily.

couple of the retaining screws. While I was in the army stationed in Germany, I used to steal ten-man "ratpacks" and stash them behind the paneling in the ablutions until

I went on leave. Apart from a few damp boxes, the stash was simple, yet effective.

The toilet cistern itself is lifted off quickly and suitably sealed items may simply be dropped in. If they are likely to interfere with the flow of water from the cistern, tape them to the inside of the unit or use sticky pads. If time permits, the ballcock mechanism that controls the level of water in the cistern can be unscrewed and items hidden within. If it is the sealed type, cut it with a hobby knife

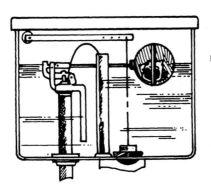

Ballcock valve assembly

and reseal with plastic tape or super glue. A small tube of glue, a roll of tape or box of sticky pads, a small pocket-clip screwdriver, and a hobby knife can all be carried easily in a jacket pocket. A Swiss army knife will do most jobs required and takes up little space.

The pipework or tubular shower curtain track can also be used, of course. Most of the shower curtain track railing is tubular, and access can be obtained by removing an end cap. Pipework will often sport a draining or unblocking plug which can be unscrewed and items inserted. Take care not to overdo the size of items, as a blocked pipe will obviously attract attention.

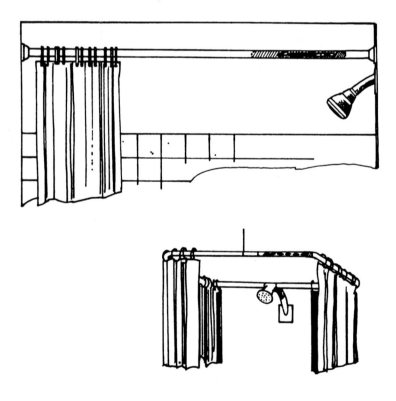

Light fittings, electric sockets, and so on can be used as shown in earlier chapters. Remember to take precautions against shock by insulating items. Use insulated screwdrivers and wear a rubber glove on the working hand.

Bathroom mirrors or the type of mirror fitted in most hotels can be removed. Lever off any plastic screwhead covers, and release the mirror from its mount. This is usually two or more small shoulders (shown below). A space exists behind the mirror to which items may be attached, or, depending on the material used for the backing, a trench can be cut out. It takes only a few

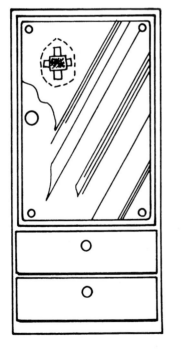

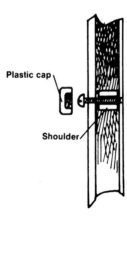

Plastic cap

Shoulder

minutes to release most mirrors, and the likelihood of cash or papers being discovered in such a place is remote. What are you looking at when you look into a mirror?

Bathroom cabinets are also mounted simply, usually with a couple of basic brackets or hooked onto a couple of screws as in the diagram below. It is a simple matter to lift the cabinet, complete with contents, off the screws and cut or scrape away a hide from the wall behind. Replace the cabinet, and that's that.

In a friend's home the bathroom will be full of toiletries and other objects that can be used to conceal items of a variety of sizes. Large jars of face cream, bubble bath, bath salts, and so on may be available. The way to use such hides is to think before you stash. Always go for large jars containing plenty of whatever. The idea is that even if the contents are used before you make a return visit to collect, plenty will remain in the container to conceal the stash. Obviously this is really most suited for small objects, but drugs, which are relatively expensive for even miniscule amounts, will find a happy home in such hides.

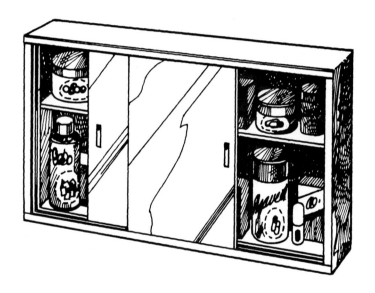

Bedding and the bed frame itself, especially in hotel rooms, can be readily used. Many modern beds of the divan type are nothing more than large wood framed boxes covered at the bottom with a layer of material. This layer can be separated and resealed with glue, or by pushing home any original staples with the heel of your shoe. The drawer divan type of bed is even quicker. Simply pull out a drawer completely and affix your valuable to the back of it as shown. Most of these drawers have a stop block on the top rail to prevent the drawer being pulled

completely out by accident. Give it a bit of jiggle and
it will come.

Material peeled back

Bottom view

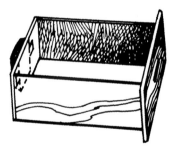

Attach item here.

If the building you are in is multistory, the top of the elevator which is accessible via an escape hatchway in its ceiling can provide useful space. When you're in a hurry items can be simply pushed up through the trap to rest on the elevator roof.

5. HINTS AND TIPS

A POINT WORTH REMEMBERING ABOUT MOST thieves, especially those house-burgling types, is that they are usually in one hell of a hurry. They want to get in and out as quickly, and with as much of your property, as possible. The same can be said of the majority of hotel thieves. Very few of them are gun carrying pros who will stop at nothing. So as to lessen the chance of your hidden valuables being found by one of these types, it is sometimes worth leaving a decoy. Deliberately leave a few dollars and a cheap watch lying around in the hotel room when you go out. Chances are the thief will grab the stuff he finds and clear out, leaving the well-hidden items safe. This technique also cuts down the risk of the hardened crook getting really annoyed at not finding anything and deciding to wait for your return in order to persuade you to part with some valuables. Nine times out of ten, he will be happy with what he can get easily, count his blessings, and go.

Believe it or not, everyone in the world has a blind spot. That means that there is a certain area within the person's field of vision that he cannot see. It may be six inches in front of him, but he will not see it. This fact can be used to great benefit in the design of camouflage wall coverings. Certain patterns would make it impossible for anyone not already aware of the locations of say, a release button, to ever find it visually. It is this principle that explains why truck mechanics often leave a wheel nut untightened after a wheel change, or why some people cannot see things that are right in front of them. I'm sure you must have been with someone looking for his car keys or the like, and you have been saying, "There! Look, in front of you," yet he still could not seem to focus on them.

You can determine your blind area by holding this page about a foot in front of your face and closing your right eye. Slowly move the book toward you while you look at the small black dot. Although, at first, you will see both the dot and the square, when the book is at your blind spot, the square will disappear. Although still there, you will no longer be able to see it. This "gap" in your visual world is *always* there! and the possibilities for exploitation of this phenomenon are tremendous.

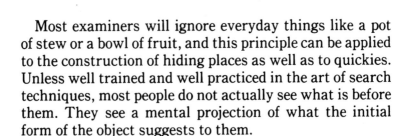

Most examiners will ignore everyday things like a pot of stew or a bowl of fruit, and this principle can be applied to the construction of hiding places as well as to quickies. Unless well trained and well practiced in the art of search techniques, most people do not actually see what is before them. They see a mental projection of what the initial form of the object suggests to them.

When you drive along a road for the first time, the surroundings seem new and interesting; the power station, the big white house that you wish you could own, and so on. Eventually, however, after you have driven the same route for a good few times, you stop seeing the power station; you don't even notice the corners in the road. You have become used to surroundings, and until the power station falls down or something else in the predictable pattern is radically changed, you will continue not seeing.

Now you can understand the importance of having things look right when using concealment techniques. A pot of stew on the stove looks right. If noticed at all, its projection is of complete normality, and suspicion does not get a foothold.

Should the unfortunate situation ever arise where you are faced with being present during a search of your property, there are a couple of things you can do to throw the examiners off the scent. The first of these is the simple and very old double bluff technique, whereby you offer as much assistance to the searching officers as possible. Open doors (except of course for those special ones), open drawers, move furniture in a helpful manner. Throughout the search insist that there is nothing there, explain how there could not be, and go into some detail as to why. For example, "No use looking there, mate, it's just an empty cupboard. I used to keep my fishing gear in there, but I sold it all a while back." The principle here is what is called a *logical perception,* which simply means that by your constant, logical statements, the guy doing the searching becomes unconsciously convinced that what you are saying is true. The same sort of thing is used by hypnotists when they repeat that you are feeling sleepy. Although there will be no conscious assistance on the part of the searcher (as there is during hypnosis), the element of unconscious persuasion is still there.

If the search has started cold but is gradually nearing your major hiding place, it will take great self-control not to either burble away like a mad thing or freeze up completely. The latter is more common. As the cupboard behind which you have a secret room is examined, you will either feel like fainting, start to sweat profusely, or begin to gibber. Any of these telltale reactions to the stress will be picked up on by an experienced search team. More often than not, one of the team will do little more than watch you for your reactions to questioning and to the search as it progresses. The oldest trick in the book used to obtain a confession (in this case as to the location of the room) is to tell the suspect that one of his colleagues has told the police about the hidden room under questioning. The bluff usually works because it is made clear that since the colleague has implicated only you, a failure on your part to cooperate will result in your taking all the stick. If you are totally sure that no one else knows the location of a room, or even that such a room exists, then you are much safer. Keep the number of people (if any) who know the location of your hiding places to a minimum. Even best friends are possible blackmail or threat victims or could fall on hard times. "Trust no one" is still a useful phrase to remember. Much as you might like to show off your custom-built hidden room, resist the temptation.

And finally a word about basic camouflage principles. By that I don't really mean that you paint the living room wall to look like a tropical sunset scene (although if you fancy doing that don't let me put you off). British camo gear is officially called D.P.M., which stands for disruptive pattern material. Its effect is to disrupt the pattern normally made by the figure of a man, helping him to lose himself among similarly colored and patterned backgrounds. Its effect is of course limited; there is no way that a single pattern can be used for every possible background. Who can tell when you might need to conceal items out in the open with only natural backgrounds as an aid?

I will limit the illustration, however, to one that is applicable to urban home-based projects. The use to which you put the example is up to your own imagination but, as with the blind spot principle, it could prove very useful.

When we look at a pattern or an object of a specific shape, our reaction to it will be either one of interest or disinterest. If we particularly like the pattern or object we will probably continue to look at it for longer than if it displeases us or does not especially interest us. Although we consider this to be a conscious, deliberate decision on our part, it rarely is. Now, someone searching for something "different"—something enough out of the ordinary to be the door to a secret room, for example, will be consciously interested in everything they see. Subconsciously, however, they will be reacting to the images before them in a predetermined way. Their experience will not be directly related to what they are actually seeing; however hard they may try, objects or patterns that appear normal will cause a block to appear between their conscious and subconscious mind. In our case the result would be a lack of suspicion of the hiding place. The most useful type of patterning for our specific purpose—in this case a wall design—is one that gives a false duration experience. That is to say, if the pattern is scrutinized for say, thirty seconds, the onlooker will feel that he has been looking at it for much longer! this adds to the effect that the visually confusing pattern is having anyway, and the search will cut short.

An ornate flower design could be a visually confusing pattern; a straight line pattern would not. Below are two patterns, extreme examples that I use to make the point. Look first at the design on the left for thirty seconds. Next look at the one on the right for *exactly* the same

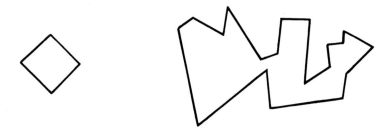

amount of time and notice how it feels as if you have been looking at the pattern on the right for much, much longer!

I served for a time in Northern Ireland with the British Army, and during house searches (of which I took part in plenty) we kicked the _____ t out of anything that looked as if it might hide something—cupboards, walls and the like were all thoroughly wrecked, er, searched! Beds and bed linen took their fair share of abuse. In fact, there were only a few places that we never bothered to examine, and these were, being honest, often the most suitable (as far as I was concerned) for hiding weapons and other contraband. I am reminded here of an episode that may interest you. It concerns house searches, and is absolutely true.

My unit in Northern Ireland had been given the job of house-searching a certain street. The searches were very high profile, and more aimed at worrying would-be gun runners and terrorists than actually turning anything up. However, several informers had targeted a house in this street as containing sympathizers and a fair amount of high explosive. We hit the property at about half-past three in the morning, tapped on the door, and whispered for the occupants to open up. They, for some reason, didn't hear us, so in we went. Everything, and I mean *everything* was searched, pulled, kicked, ripped open, and torn down, yet we came up empty-handed. Eventually the screaming occupants (screaming abuse, not with fear) and the lack of evidence persuaded us to depart. The mother stood in the doorway, baby in her arms, and hurled obscenities after us (we certainly deserved it). Anyway, over the next few weeks that property was searched a dozen times. Every time the searches came to nothing, and the screaming woman with the baby became quite a talking point. We joked about how the infant would grow up with a very colorful vocabulary indeed!

On December 24, 1974, a section of men from a different unit entered the house and one of them, after a good ear-bending from the woman, decided to get his own back by insisting that the woman remove the baby's clothes and blanket. Her attitude changed immediately, and it was soon apparent why. The little pink blanket was rigged with four hefty pockets containing the latest of what must have been a long-standing regular consignment of P.E.8 (high explosive)! The story serves to illustrate the need for thoroughness, both in concealing and searching.

On one hand, if your property is subjected to an intense, vicious search where damage is of no concern to the searcher, then you could be in for a few problems. And on the other hand, the use of innocent-looking and physically insecure objects as hiding places can be more effective than an elaborate network of secret rooms. Psychology can play a major part in the success or failure of a concealment project.

Where would *you* look for something? Where would you *not* look? Think about the last question, and try to come up with reasons for not looking somewhere. Is the area of the hide too dirty or smelly? Would that sort of thing be likely to bother the criminal type, a desperate refugee or the government employee searching on behalf of the state, who, if he finds something, will probably get a promotion or a salary increase? Can you draw the line between the impossible and the improbable?

I could go on, but I think that's enough to set you thinking. The motivation of the searcher is to be considered of paramount importance when selecting hides, so putting yourself in the other guy's shoes will help you select the best place for *your* needs.